English Homes and Housekeeping 1700–1960

English Homes
and Housekeeping
1700–1960

Barbara Megson M.A.(CANTAB)

formerly Head of History Department,
Totnes High School

Routledge & Kegan Paul Ltd. *London*

First published 1968
by Routledge & Kegan Paul Limited
Broadway House, 68-74 Carter Lane, London EC4

Phototypeset by St. Paul's
Press Limited, Malta, and
printed by Unwin Brothers Limited,
Woking and London

SBN 7100 6004 1 (p)
SBN 7100 6030 0 (c)

Contents

CONTENTS

Illustrations

ILLUSTRATIONS

Acknowledgements

In gathering the material for this book, I have been helped by a number of people to whom I wish to express warm thanks.

I am particularly grateful for the childhood memories recorded for me by Mrs. E. Burrow, Mrs. R. Jones and Miss J. O'Hare; also to Sir Alec Clegg for permission to quote from his reminiscences in a speech to the U.D.C. Association at Blackpool in June, 1966.

I also wish to thank the following authors for allowing me to quote extracts from their works: Mr. R. Church for the abstract from *Over the Bridge*, to Mr. F. Kitchin for the use of his description of a Yorkshire farm in *Brother to the Ox*, I am also indebted to the trustees of the late Flora Thompson for the quotation from *Lark Rise to Candleford* and of the late Mrs. M. Hughes for the section on shopping taken from *A London Family*: to Countrywise Books for the passages of the *Diary of a Farmer's Wife 1795–96*.

Permission has also been given by the proprietors of *Punch* for the use of Illustrations 11, 12, 16, 19, 20 and 24 and by the British Museum for Plates 2, 3, 4, 5, 6 and 10. I should also like to thank Mrs. Peirson, of Kingsbridge, for lending me the photograph of the Victorian maid (Illustration 13). I am indebted to Mr. J. F. Goodchild for finding the 'criss-cross' letter shown in Illustration 23.

Finally I wish to thank Mr. and Mrs. R. Beevers for the inspiration and encouragement to write this book.

B. E. M.

66.—This is a WIRE frame made to fit inside a pan, in which parsley or other vegetables are fried in oil. The price is 2*s.* 6*d.* and 3*s.* 6*d.*

WIRE VEGETABLE STRAINER.

The action of this familiar piece of kitchen furniture is so well known, and, if not, is so well shown in our illustration, that very little explanation is needed. When the joint is hooked on, the JACK requires winding up, which operation must be repeated once or twice during the time the meat is cooking. The price of a bottle-jack and wheel complete is 7*s.* 6*d.* and 9*s.* 6*d.*

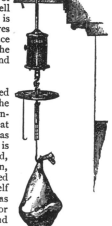

When the meat is roasting, this SCREEN is placed in front of the fire, to condense the heat as much as possible. It is made of wood, lined with tin, and is fitted with a shelf which acts as a warmer for the plates and dishes. A meat-

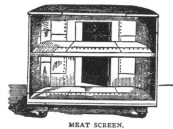

MEAT SCREEN.

screen may be purchased for 30*s.* and 52*s.*

BOTTLE-JACK AND WHEEL, WITH JOINT SUSPENDED.

67.—THE DRIPPING-PAN is the receptacle for the droppings of fat and gravy that fall from the roast meat. The pan is arranged with a well in the centre, covered with a lid ; round this well is a series of small holes, which allow the dripping to pass into the well free from cinders or ashes. When the meat is required to be basted, the lid of the well is lifted up, the dripping is free from impurities, and the surface of the joint is moistened to prevent it from scorching. The basting-ladle is half covered over at the top with a piece of metal perforated with small holes, so that, should a small piece of cinder get into the ladle it will lodge there, and *not fall on* the meat. The dripping-pans are 8*s.* 6*d.*, and the basting-ladles 1*s.* 4*d.* each.

DRIPPING-PAN AND LADLE.

FRYING-PANS are made both in iron and copper, the former, perhaps, being the most generally used. Omelet-pans are very shallow, with slanting sides, convenient for turning pancakes, ome-

FRYING-PAN.

OMELET-PAN.

lets, &c. Iron frying-pans cost from 1*s.* each ; copper omelet-pans 5*s* 6*d.* each.

1. Page 26 of the first edition of Mrs Beeton's *Book of Household Management* (1859)

Introduction

The art of housekeeping is as old as man. It caters for the basic essentials of life; food, shelter and warmth. It is so much the background of every person's life that we often take it for granted. Many history books never even mention it. This book is designed to help you to discover this story for yourselves, from the information which lies about you, waiting to be explored. The study of history is like the work of a detective; a challenge to find and understand the clues which await discovery. First let us be quite clear what we mean by housekeeping, as it is practised now. In other words, let us view our domestic surroundings with the eyes of someone who lives twenty years from now.

Go into any modern kitchen; the one at home will do splendidly. Make a list of all the equipment it contains, adding an explanation about the use of each article. Find out where it was made if possible, and what power is used to work it. Do not restrict yourself to mechanical equipment, but list the humbler housewife's workshop; its contents are designed to help her do her work and thus indicate the variety of her tasks. What would happen if, overnight, gas and electricity disappeared? Without an automatic water supply through the tap every drop of water would have to be carried from a pump in the yard or from a distant well. Any heat required would involve making a fire with wood or coal. In the old days, a shortage of wood could be disastrous, as we see in this extract, written in 1821:

... the poor take by turns, the making of fires at their houses, (in Salisbury) to boil four or five tea-kettles. What a winter life must these lead, whose turn it is not to make the fire! At Launceston in Cornwall, a man, a tradesman too, told me that the people in general could not afford to have fire in ordinary, and that he himself paid 3d for boiling a leg of mutton at another man's fire!

(Cobbett: *Rural Rides*)

Next, go into the larder and look at the labels on the

packages. Write down all the different countries on the labels. Where does most of the food come from? Try to find out why this should be. Look at the tins and cartons themselves; all weighed accurately and sealed hygienically in their containers. How did people manage when most food came in its raw state and when there was very little chance of preserving most of it for more than a few days? With goods artificially weighed and packed, we no longer have to concern ourselves with the proper seasons in which they are available. For our ancestors, it was essential to have accurate tables concerning the times of the year when different varieties of game, fish and vegetable could be obtained. An old cookery book, published in 1810 gives some good advice on such matters and on some less obvious goods also:

The price of starch depends upon that of flour; the best will keep good in a dry warm room for some years; therefore, when bread is cheap it may be bought to advantage, and covered close. Candles made in cool weather are best; and when their price and that of soap, which rise and fall together, is likely to be higher, it will be prudent to lay in the stock of both.

Few articles could be expected to last for long and needed careful storage:

Meat in a cold dry place. – Sugar and sweetmeats require a dry place; so does salt. – Candles cold, but not damp. – Dried meats, hams &c the same. – All sorts of seed for puddings, saloop, rice, &c. should be closely covered to preserve from insects. . . . Straw to lay apples on should be quite dry, to prevent a musty taste.
Large pears should be tied up by the stalk.

Shopping also had its dangers.

Though it is very disagreeable to suspect anyone's honesty, and perhaps mistakes have been unintentional; yet it is prudent to weigh meat, sugars, &c. when brought in, and compare with the charge.

Elaborate precautions were necessary to avoid being charged twice for the same goods:

A ticket should be exchanged by the cook for every loaf of bread, which when returned will show the number to be paid for; as tallies may be altered, unless one is kept by each party. Those who are served with brewer's beer, or any other articles not paid for weekly or on delivery, should keep a book for entering the dates; which will not only serve to prevent overcharges, but will show the whole year's consumption at one view. . . .

Since when, you may now ask, have we been able to rely on refrigeration? When were gas and electric cookers invented, together with automatic washers, spin-dryers, vacuum cleaners, central heating, and the preservation of foods by canning and dehydration?

Housekeeping now is simpler than it has ever been before. In the past, housekeepers carefully kept their tried recipes, for both cooking and cleaning, in note-books which were handed down from mother to daughter. In time, a few books on cookery and household management were published. One of the earliest was written by a Mrs. Hannah Glasse in 1747. Easily the most famous was that of Mrs. Beeton, which first came out in 1859, when the writer was only twenty-three years of age.

The first section of this encyclopaedic work is devoted to instructions on the daily running of the home, with or without servants. To read it is like visiting a Victorian Home in every detail. It is not surprising it was a favourite wedding present, and its modern form still is. The young housewife could consult it on every problem; from how to make afternoon calls to the bathing of the baby and the keeping of accounts. Not only does she explain how to engage servants, but the duties of each servant are described, even to instructions for the coachman on how to clean the family coach. In the margins of the recipe section are numerous wood-cut illustrations of the very latest kitchen equipment (see Illust. 1). There had been good books of this kind before, but never one so all-embracing as this.

Perhaps you think a hundred years ago a very long way off? Maybe; but many people still quite young will find, if they enquire, that their great-grandparents were very much alive when Mrs. Beeton was writing, and even in some cases their grandparents. The writer's own great-great-grandfather was born in the eighteenth century, in 1794. Her grandparents, whom she knew well, could have spoken to him and known him. Thus, in a leap one has an actual human connection with someone who lived over one hundred and sixty years ago. So even two hundred years is not so far away as one thought either. What makes 1794 seem so very remote is the speed at which life has changed and is changing. Then, a journey of twenty miles was regarded by the average person as a dangerous and difficult undertaking. People now fifty can recall the time when there was no radio, let alone television. Others of seventy well remember when horse transport was the only means of travel on the roads. Railways were the equivalent of jet propulsion and aeroplanes were not invented.

Such had been the changes during the lifetime of an old lady of 90 as, in 1965, she recalled her childhood more than eighty years ago:

School was one and a quarter miles away and I walked there twice a day, coming home at dinner time. The midday meal was the main meal and father was there most days — he used a tricycle to cover his (rate) collection area. Food was plain but good and plentiful. Vegetables and fruit were grown in the garden. Milk had to be fetched from a farm a mile away — often my job before I left for school. Butcher and baker and an occasional fishmonger called (with horse and cart). Mother did not bake her own bread.

Butter came from the farm. Shop butter was only for emergency use. Cooking was done on a range in the main room. The fire was in the centre with an oven on one side and a large boiler (with a tap) on the other. One of the daily chores was drawing water from the well and filling the boiler which must on no account be allowed to run dry. Wood was plentiful to keep the fire going but we also bought coal at £1 a ton.

A large iron pot suspended over the fire was the indispensable cooking utensil, for by careful timing, meat, vegetables and puddings could all be cooked in this and be ready to serve together. Hooks over the fire could take kettle and pans too.

Saturday night was bath night with the fire stoked up and a large zinc bath in front of it. After baths were finished Mother prepared in advance for Sunday doing everything possible to lessen Sunday labour. One hardship was visiting the privy at the bottom of the garden on a cold winter's day; another, walking to school in bad weather — there were no modern raincoats then.

The quality of life lived by this lady as a child had much in common with children hundreds of years before. She has lived to see the modern kitchen we have just examined. It is the purpose of this book to help you to discover how, as well as why, such remarkable changes have come about in our lives.

However fascinating it may be, a study of housekeeping without reference to the broader picture of the times, is meaningless. The work of the housewife is affected by many events, outside her home, whether or not she is aware of them. Government taxes can affect food prices as much as bad harvests; the shortage of goods in an island during a major war inspires improvisations and inventions to produce substitutes which, when developed, may have far-reaching results for her long after the war is over. Before beginning a detailed study, therefore, we must get a general idea of the period in which we are working.

2. Cottage industry. One room for living and working. Linen making in County Down in the reign of George III.

(*Engraved from a painting by W. Hincks*)

Notice the single large cooking pot over the fire.

The Historical Background

England on the Verge of Revolution: 1700–1815

One   The Countryside

In 1700, most Englishmen lived by and on the land. The methods of farming and the lives of the ordinary people had changed little for centuries. Bad roads ensured the almost total isolation of the village, whose customs, jealously guarded, were often distinctive to it alone. In many places farming was still carried on in the medieval three-field system, with the time-honoured custom that the villagers might use the common land for grazing their animals and the dead wood off it as a source of fuel. They were soon to be reminded, in a brutal way, that these so-called 'common rights' were originally privileges, graciously allowed by the Lord of the Manor, to whom the land really belonged. Until that time, the old way of life continued.

Let us reconstruct a typical eighteenth century village. Fortunately, there are a number of accounts, written early in the century, which give us a vivid idea of our ancestors' lives. Although one should always seek history as far as possible in the accounts of actual people, the first quotation here will be taken from a fictitious description, written at the time, of a typical character.

The leading personality of the village was the Squire, the descendant of the old Lord of the Manor. As the most substantial landowner, most of the villagers were his tenants, which gave him much power over them. In addition, many of them worked as labourers on his land which made him their employer as well. The good Squire was the father of the village; a bad one could make the lives of his people a misery. In addition to the direct relation to them as landlord and master, he was usually the local magistrate, appointed the parson and drilled the local militia. Early in the century, two essayists, Addison and Steele, set out in the *Coverley Papers*, to describe the ideal Squire. A charming and vigorous character emerges:

He is now in his fifty-sixth year, cheerful, gay and hearty. Keeps a good house both in town and country; a great lover of mankind; but there is such a mirthful cast in his behaviour, that he is rather beloved than esteemed. His tenants grow rich, his servants look satisfied, all the young women profess to love him, and the young men are glad of his company; when he comes into a house he calls the servants by their names, and talks all the way upstairs to a visit.

He went to Church himself and saw that the rest of the village did also, but there is a different kind of squire:

The fair understanding between Sir Roger and his chaplain and their mutual concurrence in doing good, is the more remarkable, because the next village is famous for the differences and contentions that rise between the parson and the 'squire, who live in a perpetual state of war. The parson is always preaching at the 'squire, and the 'squire, to be revenged on the parson, never comes to church. . . . In short, matters are come to such an extremity, that the 'squire has not said his prayers either in public or private this half-year; and that the parson threatens him, if he does not mend his manners, to pray for him in the face of the whole congregation.

(Addison)

A cottager lived a very precarious existence. Even in good times, he lived very poorly. Without the charitable ministrations of the Gentry, he and his family would often have starved. Charity to their poorer neighbours was an accepted duty of all the well-to-do, especially for the wives and daughters of landowners. Visiting the poor had its tragic, but also its amusingly human moments:

March 12th 1796.
John went to church by himself yesterday, while I went to Emma Short's cottage to wash her. I combed her hair, which was very lumpy, and also wiped the baby's face and made it tidy and comfortable, there being no-one else to do it.

I found the husband sitting by the fire and the house floor very dirty. I made him get the mop and pail of water and stood by while he cleaned, rating him soundly, but la! he put as much water on his small clothes as on the floor. . . . I told him to keep it clean until his wife was up to do it, but I doubt if he will.

(*Diary of a Farmer's Wife*, 1796–97)

In addition, she had taken sheets and a blanket, and milk for the invalid, but

I did not tell John of my giving her the sheets and blanket, him being a mere man, so it is not wise to do so, yet I could but think how much better off I be to have a good bed to lie upon and plenty of vittels of my inside. I should not like to live in a hovel like Emma Short.

The labourer's supplies came from several sources. He would hold several strips in the common fields where crops were grown, and would also work on the Squire's land, for which he received a very small payment. To eke out, he would keep a pig, and perhaps a goat or cow on the local common. His wife had a vegetable garden and kept hens. The children went out to work almost as soon as they could run. In addition the whole family used any spare time available in the spinning of wool and weaving of coarse cloth. The women, especially the unmarried daughters, spun the wool which the father would weave in the evenings, hence the term "spinsters". The cloth would then be used to make clothes for the family, but more usually would be sold to the clothier's agent. The standard of living in such a home was very poor indeed, especially in a remote country district. See Illust. 2.

John Watson had been brought up in Northumberland and he remembered well how his poor neighbours had lived then.

. . . The life of the fell folk must have been very lonely in winter. They rose and went to bed with the sun, their only artificial lights being made from rushes and mutton fat. Among the shippons [cow-houses] in winter the candles were manufactured in old-fashioned horn lanterns which were manufactured by themselves. There were no markets for the milk and butter, and so the former was converted into cheese, mostly of a very poor quality. At this period (1780) the labouring classes were badly housed; they subsisted chiefly on porridge of oatmeal, or dressed barley boiled in milk, with the addition of meal-bread, butter, and a very small quantity of salted meat. This diet told terribly upon the poorer population in spring: for ague set in with painful regularity.

(Northumberland, described by John Watson in *Annals of a Quiet Valley*)

If, as later happened, any one of their means of livelihood were taken from them, they were ruined and faced with the Workhouse. Here is an account, written in 1787, by the Rev. David Davies, the Rector of Barkham in Berkshire, of how his people lived.

In visiting the labouring families of my Parish, as my duty led me, I could not observe but with concern, their mean and distressed condition. I found them in general but indifferently fed; badly clothed; some children without shoes and stockings, very few put to school; and most families in debt to little shopkeepers. Yet I could not impute the wretchedness that I saw either to sloth or wastefulness. For I knew that the farmers were careful that the men should not want employment; and had they been given to drinking, I am sure I should have heard of it, and I commonly found the women, when not working in the fields, well occupied at home; seldom indeed earning money, but baking their bread, washing and mending their garments, and rocking the cradle.

This is the kind of description which, if you are lucky, you may find for your own district. You will probably find greater details concerning the exact diet that such people ate.

In addition to the Squire, there were often in every district a few substantial farmers. Like the Squire, they employed local labour on their land. Unlike him, however, they ran their farms on what was known as the 'living-in system'. All the unmarried boys and girls employed on the farm lived in the attics of the farmhouse and were fed by the farmer's wife. Howitt, a well known popular writer in the 1830's, gives this pleasant description of the friendly relations that could exist in such a farmhouse:

4

At night, the farmer takes his seat on the settle, under the old wide chimney — his wife has her work-table set near — the 'wenches' darning their stockings, or making up a cap for Sunday, and the men sitting on the other side of the hearth, with their shoes off. He now enjoys of all things, to talk over his labour and plans with his men. . . . . .

The Labourer, says Howitt,

. . . was regarded as one of the farmer's own family, for whose good conduct and appearance the master was in some degree accountable and for whose success in life, if he conducted himself properly, he was never entirely indifferent.

There were many advantages to this system. As far as the labourers and 'wenches' were concerned, they were better fed and looked after than they ever would be again in their lives. As soon as they were able to get a cottage and marry, the dismal struggle for existence, described earlier, would close in upon them. It is not surprising that the age of marriage was often over thirty among cottagers. In addition, girls trained by a farmer's wife were well grounded in every aspect of the then complicated art of running a home. The farmer's wife as well as her duties in the house, usually took responsibility for the dairy. She and her maids would lift and carry heavy cheeses and butter cans for market; the wife was expected to run her household on the profits she made in this way. Market day was the signal for great activity:

14th February 1797
Yesterday we were very busy washing clothes, baking bread and other oddments; later I and John's Mother went to take my butter and eggs to sell. The roads are very muddy so that we bumped a good deal and had a lot of trouble to get along with old Dobbin. I always like to go to the market: it is very nice to get into company sometimes. I sold my butter for sevenpence a pound and sixpence a score for the eggs, which are now dearer, and so adds more money to my stocking. I bought a ribbon for Sarah's hair and a ginger bread man, as well as one for Carter's wife, and a packet of tobacco for John, with various other things we need. Then we went home, it being a dirty day and very cold so we were glad

to get back to my warm kitchen, where Sarah had a nice hot meal ready for our return, and a hot noggin of spiced wine to warm our insides. . . .

(Diary of a Farmer's Wife, 1796–97)

Sarah was the maidservant. The maids helped her with her chickens, bees, brewing and the salting of meat for the winter. Preparations for the winter had to be gigantic.

As yet (1780) the art of fattening cattle was but little understood . . . The stock which was fed in autumn was killed off by Christmas, and, with the exception of veal, scarcely any fresh meat appeared in the markets before the ensuing midsummer. This dearth the more substantial yeoman and manufacturers provided against by curing a quantity of beef at Martinmas, part of which was pickled in brine, the rest dried in the smoke of capacious chimneys.

On Sundays the farmer's wives boiled a huge piece of meat from the brine-tub, which on that day was served hot. From that day as long as the joint lasted it came up cold, relish being given to it by the addition of oatmeal pudding. Hogs were slaughtered in great numbers between Christmas and Candlemas, the flesh being converted into bacon, which, with dried beef and mutton, afforded a change in spring.

The only fresh provisions of winter consisted of eggs, poultry, geese, and ill-fed veal, the calves being then carried to market when two or three weeks old. In some of the northern rivers salmon was very abundant, and sold at twopence a pound.

(John Watson: *Annals of a Quiet Valley*)

Reference was made in this last extract to Yeomen. These were small but independent farmers who usually worked their own land but since there was often very little of it, the responsibility of making it pay must often have been very heavy.

Two   Change in the Village

Such is a very general picture of the countryside before the revolutionary changes which were already, in some parts, well under way. The

3. Farmer Giles and his wife showing off their daughter Betty
to their neighbours on her return from school.
   (*Cartoon by James Gillray, 1809*)
**Can you write the sort of conversation the neighbours would
have afterwards? What signs of wealth are there in this
room?**

old farming methods were barely adequate even when the only object
of the farmer was to meet his own and his family's immediate needs.
For many reasons, from the late seventeenth century, there was an
increasing demand for greater food production. Towns were
expanding and did not produce any food for themselves, so they
turned to the farmer for greater quantities.

William III, when he became King in 1688, had passed an Act
through Parliament by which a bounty of 5/- would be paid for every
quarter of wheat (504 lbs) exported abroad. The wars in Europe
meant that other countries were willing and anxious to buy any
surplus food from England. Encouraged by the certainty of selling
what they grew, the wealthier farmers, who could afford to, had
made many experiments to find more efficient and scientific methods

of production. They were rewarded with great success, but it was clear from the beginning that, as the demand for foodstuffs increased, the new farming could only be operated if the old system of open fields, on which the peasant farmed his own strips, gave way to larger farms. This led to the enclosure by Act of Parliament, first of the common land and later of the big fields. The large farmers were delighted with the results. Their profits and rents rose magnificently. For the cottager, it was another story.

'Has Meriden Common been long enclosed?' asked John Byng of a Warwickshire labourer.
'Ah, lackaday, Sir, that was a sad job; and ruin'd all us poor volk: and those who then gave into it now repent it.'
'Why so?'
'Because we had our garden, our bees, our share of a flock of sheep, the feeding of our geese; and could cut turf for our fuel. – Now all that is gone!'*

(1788)

What this meant to a labourer in Sussex was well described by the same author thus:

How wretched do the miseries of a cottage appear! (and this was only of comparative distress); want of food, want of fuel, want of clothing! Children perishing of an ague! and an unhappy mother unable to attend to, or relieve their wants, or assuage their pains; nor to allow time sufficient even for melancholy father (perhaps a shepherd) pinch'd by cold, and pining with despair, returns at evening close to a hut devoid of comfort, or the smallest renovation of hope; for no longer are left the fost'ring forgiving hand of his landlord, or the once bountiful buttery of the manor house, to apply to.

---

*The shortage of fuel had another serious result: bread was no longer baked at home. Bakeries were to be found in most villages in southern England after 1815. The bakers prided themselves on making the fine white bread which had become fashionable in London over a century earlier. The fine milling needed to make white flour removed the germ from the wheat, the most nourishing part of the grain. Only in the North was it possible for the housewife to continue to make her own good whole meal grains.

The old 'living-in' system of the big farm had clearly gone. The rich farmers no longer wanted the trouble or expense of looking after their workmen under their roof. Cobbett wrote indignantly:

The farmer's wife stuck up in a place she calls a *parlour*, with, if she have children, the 'young ladies and gentlemen' about her . . . a dinner brought in by a girl that is perhaps better 'educated' than she . . . the house too neat for a dirty-shoed carter to be allowed to come in-to. (See Illust. 3)

Why do not farmers now *feed* and *lodge* their work-people, as they did formerly? Because they cannot keep them *upon so little* as they give them in wages.

Despite their loss of common land and their strips, the labourers were paid no more by the farmers than previously. Their plight was as desperate as it could well be. Small wonder that some fell into the state of despair and apathy described by the agricultural journalist, Arthur Young, in one of his tours round the country:

Go to an alehouse kitchen of an old enclosed country, and there you will see the origin of poverty and poor rates. For whom are they to save? (such are their questions). For the parish? If I am diligent, shall I have land for a cow? If I am frugal, shall I have half an acre of potatoes? You offer no motives; you have nothing but a parish officer and a workhouse!

Struck by the poverty of their local workers, and horrified by the resulting rise in the poor rates, which as landowners they had to pay, a number of Justices of the Peace met in Speen, in Berkshire in 1795 to consider the position. They decided to keep the dreaded workhouses as empty as possible by helping the labourer out, week by week, if he could show that his wage was insufficient to support him and his family. His case was to be decided according to the number of children in his family and the price of bread in the area for that week. This scheme was quickly adopted by many districts all over the country and became known as "the Speenhamland system'. It had many defects. No matter how hard he worked the labourer would never be paid enough to support him. This did not encourage

4. A country cottage in 1808.
(Engraving, 'The Cut Finger', 1808)
**What differences can you see here from the earlier cottage
in Illust. 2.**

him to do his best work. The farmers, who all kept wages down since
the labourer would still survive, were surprised to find that the rates
went up! It continued to be used, however, until 1834, when the
Poor Law Amendment Act swept it away.

With all its faults, the Speenhamland system did prevent total
starvation among the peasantry affected by the Enclosure movement.
They also received temporary relief out of the national emergency
caused by the great war against Napoleon. This shrewd enemy found

10

5. The troubles of a farm labourer in 1795. Prices were up: wages had not risen.

(*Cartoon by James Gillray, 1795*)

Notice the way the food was displayed in the shop.

the really weak link in England's armour. In 1775 the Corn Bounty had been paid for the last time. Why? The reason is significant. England's towns had now reached such a size that all the farmers' surplus was needed to feed the townsmen. Never again was England to be a self-sufficient island. She would always be dependent in future on food from abroad. Like Kaiser Wilhelm and Hitler after him, Napoleon saw that, if he struck at our food convoys, he might have a chance of starving us out of the war, as a siege of a castle often did in earlier times. As a result, every inch of cultivable land in Britain was ploughed up and sown, even if it was poor land and produced comparatively little crop. Every little helped. The labourer, if he did not go into the army, found work was once more to be obtained in the fields. Such was the emergency that even women were to be seen working on the land. Miss Mitford, in *Our Village*, has a vivid description of these women hard at work beansetting. Until the war was over then, the countryman, hard as his life was, could generally keep going (see Illust. 4). In the obvious shortage of food, however, prices rocketed, and he was still not paid a living wage. It was not the first time he had been faced with the tragic dilemma which had been illustrated by Gillray in a cartoon of 1795 (see Illust. 5).

To the ignorant and isolated countryman, the changes which brought such misery were inexplicable. To understand them, one must turn to the life of the eighteenth century town.

Three   Town Life

Towns are centres for trade, manufacture and government. All three activities were prospering when Daniel Defoe toured Britain in the early years of the century. He was shocked by the increasing luxury of life in the towns, especially in London. When there is plenty of money, goods sell fast. The life of a London tradesman was a busy and rewarding one:

Rise at 5; counting-house till 8; then breakfast on toast and Cheshire cheese; in his shop for two hours then a neighbouring coffee house for news; shop again, til dinner at home (over the shop) at 12 on a 'thundering joint'; 1 o'clock on Change; 3, Lloyd's Coffee House for business; shop again for an hour; then another coffee house (not Lloyd's) for recreation, followed by 'sack shop' to drink with apprentices, till home for a 'light supper' and so to bed, 'before Bow Bell rings nine'.

(quoted from a Diary of 1706 by Sir G. M. Trevelyan
in *English Social History*)

Defoe also exclaimed at the money spent on building and furnishing shops, not to mention the fancy goods they stocked:

First let him reckon up all the houses that are now to let and are actually shut up, and then let him set aside all the pastry cooks, coffee houses, perriwig makers, cane chair men, brandy shops and the like, whose places of trade used to be found only in back streets, lanes and allies are fittest for such places . . . we find the most noble shops in the city taken up with the valuable utensils of the tea table . . . two thousand pounds reckoned a small stock in copper pots and lacker'd kettles, and the very fitting up of one of these brazen people's shops, &c, costs above £500 sterling . . . This certainly shows the increase of our trade . . .

(1713)

The City housewife, if she had the means, had no need to be self-sufficient as did her country sister (see Illust. 6). In London shops, many exotic articles were already to be found, brought from India by the Great East India Company. Enterprising shop-keepers had already set up hot-pie shops* and quite early in the century one reads complaints of lazy wives who, instead of cooking for themselves, as good wives should, bought hot, ready-made food. Many sent their own cakes and meat to be baked at a commercial bakehouse, a custom which continued as late as 1848, as shown in a Christmas picture by John Leech (see Illust. 7).

The wealthy tradesmen and professional families lived dignified

---

* Later, in the 1850's, with the coming of railways and deep-sea trawlers, fresh fish could be brought inland quickly and the hot-pie shops became fish-and-chip shops.

6. A London milk-maid in the eighteenth century.
   (*Engraving from a painting by F. Wheatley, 1793*)
**Notice the shoulder-yoke to bear the weight of the heavy
cans, and the measure-ladle held in her hand.**

7. A London bakehouse on Christmas Day 1848.
   (*Cartoon by John Leech, 1848*)

What kind of life do you think the people in this picture lived?

and comfortable lives in the well-proportioned red brick houses which were a feature of the new squares and streets which we still admire today as 'Georgian' architecture. On June 12th, 1770, Dr Knyveton, a fashionable London Doctor, wrote about his new house in his diary thus:

June 12th: Am decided to move into a new house, which Elizabeth and I today inspected in Queen Street, Golden Square, our present home is too cramped, and the children, by God's mercy, may improve in fresh sur-

C

roundings. The parish are putting down new clean paving stones, and sundry merchant's signes are now being replaced by numbers only. But when ours receives its number, I trust it will already be known simply as 'The Doctor's' It is a pleasant airy old fashioned stone and red brick structure, with long formal windows and a Palladian porch; a square of narrow sooty garden behind, and a coach-house backing on to a mews. On the ground floor, two rooms divided by a broad passage, a closet, and a kitchen; the two rooms and the closet will furnish yr. obdt. with lecture rooms and office; on the first floor, two large rooms and two small; the two large will be a dining room and a salon — for one has a fine copy of the fireplace by the Adams brothers — and Elizabeth has taste. The two small rooms are to be our bedroom and nursery; above are garrets for the domestics. All is in good repair, the roof sound, plenty of additional water from a deep well in the garden, and little re-decorating to be done. Elizabeth is all excitement, and I must confess I too am agog to cast anchor in this new and pleasant harbour.

August 4th: We are settled in our new house, and it is very fine. There is a shelf for books in a cupboard, and a fine broad table and strong mahogany chairs in my office; but the chief glory lies in the two rooms on the first floor — the drawing room with a steel fire grate, two tall gilt mirrors, a red and blue carpet, a settee and armchairs of mahogany upholstered with needlework, a glass chandelier! and on the walls, two large panels of china wall paper, a gift from Mr Brodie, painted by hand in brilliant colours with flowers and birds; a very rare and precious novelty; the curtains caused Elizabeth deep thought, but after much quaint knitting of her small brow, and consulting of me as to expense, they are now of silk damask in crimson, blue and green with a gilt border, rather an expense! but a good long term investment, as the mercer assures us they will stand years of wear.

Our dining room has a fine mahogany table, a mahogany sideboard with a marble top, and a folding leather screen, whilst the bedroom is all gold and green, with a figured velvet overspread and white satin curtains with pink ribbon bindings!

The pine panelling in the hall, its lantern, and the pine panelling of the ground floor rooms all scrubbed and polished; the floors waxed, plenty of candles in the candle-cupboard in the hall, and everything of brass or metal, from door handles to kitchen pans, scrubbed and polished till they gleam like silver . . .

8. A typical London street scene of the early nineteenth century, showing Georgian-style houses.

Such a house would resemble one in Illust. 8. It is significant that it belonged to a doctor, for this was an age of great medical improvements, and the status of doctors was improving with their higher fees and the demand for their skilled services. As a result of the discoveries made at this time, many lives were saved which would previously have been lost. One is inclined to forget how terrible the mortality rate was among our ancestors. Many children were born, but you had to be tough to survive to adulthood. Many mothers died in child-birth. In 1760 one in every fifteen new-born babies died at the London Lying-in Hospital. Doctor Knyveton, whose diary you have just been reading, was a midwife, one of the first qualified men to take the study of child-birth seriously. Before him, women were usually attended by dreadful old women who often

17

did both mother and child much harm through the superstitious practices they used. There were many such women still alive and working when Dickens wrote about Sarah Gamp, the midwife in *Martin Chuzzlewit*, a hundred years later. As a result of the lives saved by doctors, the population increased rapidly at this time. Previously, there had always been a fear lest the numbers of the population fall. By 1798, however, we hear of a clergyman, called Malthus, alarmed at the rise in numbers, prophesying starvation if they continue to increase at this rate. What, one wonders, would he have thought if he had known that, in the Census returns of 1961, over fifty three million people were found to be living in Great Britain. So far, we have not starved, though the provision of homes and amenities for such a large number of people is a problem much in the minds of sociologists and planners for the future.

Another significant fact we should notice about the doctor's new home is that it is intended to be run with the help of servants. Of these there are plenty, and more were coming into the City every day from the country. Arthur Young, writing in his *Farmers Letters* in 1771, gives one explanation:

To find fault with good roads would have the appearance and paradox of absurdity; but it is nevertheless a fact that giving the power of expeditious travelling depopulates the Kingdom. Young men and women in the country villages fix their eyes on London as the last stage of their hope. They enter into service in the country for little else but to raise money enough to go to London, which was no such easy matter when a stage coach was four or five days in creeping a hundred miles.

The old bumpy roads, mentioned by the Farmer's wife, not only broke eggs on the way to the market, but also the new pottery and china, made in the Midlands in great quantities for the whole of England and for overseas trade. Trade needed good roads to convey raw materials to the factories and to take the manufactured goods to the towns for sale. The towns, as they grew larger, also needed more food, brought in from the country by road. It is not surprising,

18

therefore, that the eighteenth century saw a great improvement in the building of roads and of their extension all over the island. Not only goods, but people were now able to travel faster, and small villages and towns which had hitherto lived quite out of touch with the news of national events, were now brought into contact with a wider world. One writer at the time compared 'the cautious steps of our Forefathers', with the 'almost Winged Expedition' now possible.

Changes in farming, industry and transport were closely connected. As the demand for goods increased, machinery was invented to supply it more quickly in larger quantities. In the days of hand weaving and spinning, it was possible to carry out the processes in one's one cottage, but the new machinery was often too big for that and had to be set up in large workshops; thus factories came into being. William Radcliffe, a man who lived in the North where these changes came about, looked back in 1828 to the 1770's and described the effects of the new changes on the community he knew:

In the year 1770 the land in our township was occupied by between fifty to sixty farmers . . . . . and out of these . . . . there were only six or seven who raised their rents directly from the produce of their farms; all the rest got their rent partly from some branch of trade, such as spinning and weaving woollen, linen, or cotton. The cottagers were employed entirely in this manner, except for a few weeks in the harvest . . . . .

Cottage rents at the time, with convenient loom-shop and a small garden attached, were from one and half to two guineas per annum. The father of a family would earn from eight shillings to half a guinea at his loom, and his sons six or eight shillings each per week; but the great sheet-anchor of all cottages and small farms was the labour attached to the hand-wheel . . . . . and . . . . . every person from the age of eight to eighty years . . . . . (could) . . . . . earn their bread, say one to three shillings per week, without going to the parish.

From the year 1770 to 1788 a complete change had gradually been effected in the spinning of yarns . . . new weavers' cottages filled, and when in full work the weekly circulation of money, as the price of labour only, rose to five times the amount ever before experienced in this subdivision, every family bringing home weekly 40, 60, 80, 100, or even 120 shillings per week.

This was the effect of the expansion of the cotton industry in one district in the North. As long as there was a demand for the goods, there was plenty of work for all and a boom period existed. The weavers experienced a more luxurious life than they had ever known:

Both as cottagers and small farmers, even with three times their former rents, they might be truly said to be placed in a higher state of wealth, peace, and godliness, by the great demand for, and high price of, their labour, than they had ever before experienced. Their dwellings and small gardens clean and neat, – all the family well clad – the men with each a watch in his pocket and the women dressed to their own fancy, – the Church crowded to excess every Sunday, – every house well furnished with a clock in elegant mahogany or fancy case, – handsome tea services in Staffordshire ware, with silver or plated sugar tongs and spoons, – Birmingham potteries, and Sheffield wares for necessary use and ornament, wherever cupboard or shelf could be placed *to show them off*, – many cottage families had their cow, paying so much for the summer's grass, and about a statute acre of land laid out for them in some croft or corner, which they dressed as a meadow for hay in the winter. (*Radcliffe*)

Four Hardship in the Towns

Times were not always so good. England was the first country ever to experience such changes as industrialisation and the social conditions which accompanied them. Booms alternated with slumps, when too few goods were sold and the factories had to slow down their production. This in turn meant that many people were 'laid off' work until better times should come and the demand revive. Unemployment was also caused by the failure to synchronise mechanical improvements. If a new machine for spinning produced so much yarn that the weavers could not keep up with the spinners, the spinners would find themselves out of work until the weavers caught up with them. Sometimes the reverse happened and the weavers found themselves out of work, waiting for the spinners. There was a serious slump, when large numbers of people found themselves unemployed, about once every ten years, all through the nineteenth century. Then poverty and hardship, as bitter as any in the country, came into the towns.

Industry was given an immense push forward by the Napoleonic wars. As always in such emergencies, all the country's resources were directed towards the war effort. It is said Napoleon once referred to us as 'a nation of shopkeepers', but his scorn overlooked the great power our increasing wealth gave us. It is also fact that some of his troops marched into battle dressed in good British broadcloth, for it had no rival throughout the world! So great was the need for wool cloth, that most of what was produced at that time was reserved for military use. The cotton mills had just then developed a process for the making of fine muslin, like that produced in India and so much admired by fashionable ladies. Fortunately for the war effort, women's dresses had recently taken on a loose flowing look, supposed to be like those of Ancient Greece (see Illust. 9). Led by Paris, and regardless of the English climate, women rushed to clothe themselves in clinging folds of muslin, a fashion eagerly encouraged by the government, with its eye on the heavy cloth it needed for uniforms.

In those days, a war affected Englishmen very indirectly as a rule. You might have a brother at the Front, but you yourself continued to live a normal life. More food had to be grown on the land and, if the harvest were bad, you might feel hungry since there was nothing to be expected from abroad. Money was raised for the war-effort through taxes. Among the objects affected were candles, farm horses, sheepdogs, leather, malt and barley. The rise in price of the last two articles dealt a severe blow to beer as the traditional drink for all. Until the 1780's every cottage and farm had brewed its own; water was not usually fit to drink in its normal state, and even children drank what was known as 'small beer'. The average

9. Muslin dresses in 1804.
Note the high waists and shapeless gloves.

workman drank huge quantities every day; about two quarts in winter and five in summer. Beer and cheese was the old equivalent of the modern 'tea break'. During the war, and earlier in some cases, tea became the national English drink. The East India Company had a monopoly of import and brought it direct from India, which made

10. 'John Bull's Progress'.
I John Bull happy   II John Bull going to the wars
III John Bull's property in danger   IV John Bull's glorious return
   (*Cartoon by James Gillray, 1793*)
A bitter comment on the effects of the Napoleonic war on ordinary people.

it comparatively cheap. Great ladies chose delicate blends, but for the poor, it was evidently a matter of economy, to judge from this comment by the Rev. David Davies on his parishioners, in 1787:

Beer has been these many years far beyond their ability to use in common . . . . . Tea (with bread) furnishes one meal for a whole family every day, at no greater expense than about one shilling a week at an average . . . . You exclaim Tea is a luxury. If you mean fine hyson tea, sweetened with refined sugar, and softened with cream, I readily admit it to be so. But *this* is not the tea of the poor. Spring water, just coloured with a few leaves of the lowest priced tea, and sweetened with the brownest sugar, is the luxury for which you reproach them.

English history has been tranquil by comparison with European countries because of her island position in the natural moat of the Channel. Real fear was felt during the Napoleonic War when a genuine threat of invasion was recognised. Not since the days of the Armada had we stood in such peril, civilians and soldiers alike. No wonder many of our ancestors at that time quaked in their beds as they thought of the possible arrival of 'Boney' and his men; just as many of us did, in similar circumstances in 1940–41. On both occasions, the threat never materialised.

Not until after the war did most people realise that the old England, which had begun to change in the eighteenth century, was gone forever. Some, like Cobbett, bitterly regretted it, but in vain (see Illust. 10). Once set in motion, the wheels of progress marched on, heedless, of many other changes which automatically came with them. Others, like the great inventors and factory owners, hailed the nineteenth century as the age of progress. Let us now see how the general public was affected.

Five   1815 : Post War England

The Battle of Waterloo (1815) marked the end of twenty years of fighting for England. As in the 1939–45 War, England had at times been the sole unconquered nation left to fight the common enemy. In both periods, her resources were strained to the uttermost. Foreigners, visiting the country for the first time for many years, expected to find her exhausted and ruined. On the contrary, in response to the demands of the war effort, she had developed her industries, like hot-house growths, and a prosperous factory-owning class was growing richer and more numerous every day. One Frenchman, surveying the scene with surprise, wrote in 1816:

Everywhere throughout impoverished Europe, the commerce of England seemed to recede before our victorious banners. We imagined that Great Britain, exhausted, was on the brink of ruin. But while our sight was darkened by the smoke of a noble incense of glory, unlooked for opulence overflowed with its treasures for the British Empire. The rivers were not wide enough to contain all the ships, and fewer years sufficed for a few individuals to execute and construct, at their expense, the docks which receive the trading fleets of the two hemispheres, than it required for the triumphant Government of France to erect some of the quays of the Seine.

One of the wonders of the capital in 1815 was to be found at Westminster. Gas lighting had been installed on Westminster Bridge in the previous year, though it took some years before it was generally used to light people's homes.

A new age of prosperity began. England was not to have to defend herself for another ninety nine years and was free to develop into the most powerful and wealthy country ever known before the nineteenth century. The men who held the power in 1815 were the landowners who alone had the right to elect and stand for Parliament. Their first thought, at the end of the war, was to give themselves relief from the Income Tax which had been essential during the war. It had been introduced as an emergency measure only and was regarded as an intolerable invasion of a man's personal liberties. Accordingly, they abolished it in 1816. It was a short-sighted policy, for you cannot rule without money, and some other source had to be found.

Sidney Smith, a famous wit of the period, described the resulting state of affairs:

The price of glory was taxes on the ermine which decorates the judge and the rope which hangs the criminal — on the poor man's salt and the rich man's spices — on the brass nails of the coffin and the ribands of the bride . . . The schoolboy whips his taxed top, the beardless youth manages his taxed horse with a taxed bridle on a taxed road, and the dying Englishman, pouring his medicine which has paid seven per cent into a spoon which has paid fifteen per cent, flings himself back upon his chintz bed, which has paid twenty-two per cent, and expires into the arms of the apothecary who has paid a licence of a hundred pounds for the privilege of putting him to death.

The most serious burden for the poor came about through the action of the same men: this was the high price of bread. During the war, the farmers had been the only corn-suppliers for bread: in the shortage they had been able to make immense profits, through charging high prices, and were determined to keep this advantage. Accordingly, they passed the Corn Laws of 1815. These forbade the import of cheap foreign corn until the English product reached the price of 80/- per quarter (504 lbs). This measure resulted in the cost of a large quartern loaf rising from 10d to 1/2d. The poor man relied on bread as his main food and it is not surprising that there were many hunger riots, made worse by post-war unemployment, in the years after 1815 (see Illust. 11).

In really bad times the poor man was sorely tempted to poach for game, a form of stealing from the large landowner. With no police force the eighteenth century had only one answer to this: savage

11. The home of the rick-burner, 1844. Men reached a state of despair where only violent destruction seemed likely to attract the attention of the government.
   (*Cartoon by John Leech in Punch*)

penalties if the man were caught by the Gamekeeper. Transportation was also a common punishment. The injustices which resulted are well demonstrated by Sidney Smith, writing in 1823:

27

One man is transported for stealing three bones and a pot of sausages; in the next berth to him on board is a young surgeon, who has been engaged in the mutiny at the Nore; the third man is for extorting money . . . . then comes a man who set his house on fire to cheat the Phoenix Office; and lastly, that most glaring of all human villains, a poacher, driven from Europe, wife and child, by thirty lords of manors, for killing a partridge.

'One might as well be hanged for a sheep as a lamb' was literally true, until Sir Robert Peel, as Home Secretary, brought in his sweeping penal reforms in the 1820's.

Six Servants

A new and increasingly important group of society at this time was that of the rich business men and factory owners. It was a snobbish age, in which the landed aristocracy held aloof from the mere 'moneyed' class, who did everything they could to prove themselves as good as the noblemen. As the population grew, and unemployment with it, more and more servants were available for very low wages (see Illust. 12). A man's social status could be assessed by counting the number and variety of his servants. In a book written in 1825 by Mr. and Mrs. S. Adams, called *The Complete Servant*, a scale of social ranks was drawn up, based on income and the appropriate number of servants given for each.* It gives us much insight into the sharply defined ranks of society in 1825, and some startling information on how our ancestors were paid for domestic work, though it must be remembered that they were also given, as a rule, uniform, food and lodging.

There was little commercial entertainment which could be bought at a time when even their employers entertained themselves largely at home with cards, musical evenings, charades, reading and sewing. It was very common for one member of the household to read out loud a book, while the rest of the ladies sewed. In very great houses,

* (It is too long to print here and will be found in full in Appendix I, at the end of the book).

12. A Victorian cook in her kitchen.
 (*Cartoon from Punch Almanack, 1874*)

the lesser servants were employed, not to wait upon their employers, but on the senior servants. The Butler and Housekeeper presided together over the servants hall 'below stairs' in a large house and themselves lived in considerable state. In the country there were occasional parties and dances held in the servants hall, to which the servants from a neighbouring great house were sometimes invited. Given a fair-minded Butler and Housekeeper, such a life had many attractions and was much missed by those who left it.

Let us examine the Adams' table more closely. We learn that a man with as little as one hundred and fifty pounds a year could afford to keep a maid, at a wage of between ten and twelve pounds per annum. A family earning a salary of five hundred pounds a year

29

could live in style, with 'three females and one man; viz. a cook, housemaid and a nursery maid or another female servant; with a livery servant as groom and footman. A gardener occasionally'.

The home of a really rich man, with an income of four thousand pounds or more, had at least eleven females and thirteen men:

> . . . a housekeeper, cook, lady's maid, nurse, two housemaids, laundry maid, still-room maid, nursery maid, kitchen maid and scullion; with a butler, valet, house steward, coachman, two grooms, one assistant groom, two footmen, three gardeners and a labourer.

In a house of this grandeur, it was customary after a dinner party, for all the servants to line the entrance hall as the guests departed to receive a large tip from each of the diners. In large houses, this meant a gold coin and, for an impoverished guest could be a serious drawback to accepting an invitation.

The less well off the master of the house, the harder the work for the servants. Fewer were kept but the work they shared between them was still great. The worst position was easily that of the maid-of-all-work, of whom Mrs. Beeton wrote feelingly:

> . . . perhaps the only one of her class deserving of her commiseration; her life is a solitary one, and, in some places, her work is never done. She is also subject to rougher treatment than either the house or kitchenmaid, especially in her earlier career; she starts in life, probably a girl of thirteen, and the mistress's commands are the measure of the maid-of-all-work's duties.

To her, fell all the many tasks of a Victorian household, with no labour-saving devices to help her. Her day began early:

> The housemaid who studies her own ease will certainly be at her work by six o'clock in the summer, and probably half past six or seven in the winter months, earlier than this would, probably, be an unnecessary waste of coal and candles in winter.

Before the family came down to breakfast, she had to clean and light the kitchen range, open all the shutters downstairs, sweep and clean the parlour, light a fire there and lay the table for breakfast. She then swept the Hall, cleaned the door-step and brass knocker, and cleaned the boots for all those leaving the house early. She next served breakfast and had her own. After this, she aired the bedrooms, cleared and washed up the breakfast things and made the beds, for which she wore a special apron, covering her smutty one, thus keeping the beds clean. She then tackled the drawing room:

The lady of the house when there is but one servant kept, frequently takes charge of the drawing-room herself, that is to say, dusting it; the servant sweeping, cleaning windows, looking-glasses, grates, and rough work of that sort. If there are many ornaments and knick-knacks about the room, it is certainly better for the mistress to dust these herself, as a maid-of-all-work's hands are not always in a condition to handle delicate ornaments.

It is not surprising at this stage, that the girl had reached mid-morning in her long day. She was now sent to the kitchen to prepare the dinner, with the help of her mistress; after which, she laid the table, served the family and cleared up before she had her own. Having washed up, she did all the dirty chores such as cleaning the knives and the family's boots and shoes before changing into her afternoon uniform, ready to serve tea. Then she turned down the sheets and shut the bedroom windows. In addition to all this, she was expected to have a systematic routine of thoroughly cleaning out at least two rooms a day. Such a girl could not afford to waste a minute:

A bustling and active girl will always find time to do a little needlework for herself, if she lives with consistent and reasonable people. In the summer evenings she should manage to sit down for two or three hours, and for a short time in the afternoon on leisure days. A general servant's duties are so multifarious that, unless she be quick and active, she will not be able to accomplish this . . . . .

Her wage for all this activity was between nine and fourteen pounds a year 'without an extra allowance for tea, sugar and beer. £7½ to £11 where such allowances are made'.

Seven   Town Houses: The Rich

The houses which the servants looked after were as difficult to
clean as they could be. The new factories were constantly bringing
out cheap copies of furnishing which before had only been available
to the rich. The man who wished to impress his neighbours filled his
home with heavily carved furniture, tables loaded with dust-catching
ornaments and plants like the aspidistra and ferns. The fireplace
was smothered in fringed velvet and embroidered pom-poms, the
door was shrouded with a heavy curtain against draughts. The new
colour-print pictures were framed and hung all over the walls and the
new family photographs stood on the tops of furniture. Every
cushion, lace curtain and lace mat was 'worked' by a devoted army
of daughters and their mothers.

The middle class woman was a casualty of the industrial revolution. In the eighteenth century, when her husband worked at home
and they lived on the business premises, the wife often helped
the husband with his work. Large machinery has to be housed in
a factory, however, and the business and office moved into special
premises. The wife was left at home. Gradually her function became
more and more idle and ornamental. In many cases mothers did not
even bring up their own children, but handed them over to a nursemaid who presided over the nursery, which was kept well away
from the main rooms of the house, lest the noise of the children
should disturb the peaceful calm of the world downstairs (see
Illust. 13). How did these women occupy themselves? In the country,
there was always much visiting of the poor and sick in the village.
In the town, though there was much need of it, much less charitable
visiting was done. Miss Florence Nightingale, the great pioneer
nurse, witheringly referred to this activity as "soup and blanket"
charity, since it only scratched the surface of the need. She was
one of the single daughters who hated her rich, leisured life, longing
to have an outlet for her energy and talents. In 1852, two years

13. A nursemaid with her charge in 1882.

before she had her opportunity to nurse in the Crimean war, she wrote bitterly about the useless life of women of her class:

Her 'domestic duties', high-sounding words, which, for the most part, are bad habits (which she has not the courage to enfranchise herself from, the strength to break through) ... What are these duties (or bad habits) — Answering a multitude of letters which lead to nothing, from her so-called friends, keeping herself up to the level of the world that she may furnish her quota of amusement at the breakfast table; driving out her company in the carriage.

Miss Nightingale was determined and strong minded. Many of the reforms she later introduced into hospitals contributed directly to the health and well-being of ordinary people's homes.

Many women, however, enjoyed spending their days in reading, needlework, painting and playing instruments, but it is not surprising that there was a good deal of largely imaginary illness, commonly called the "vapours", among this class of women. There was too much time for gloomy and morbid thoughts. Often, she knew little or nothing about the running of the home of which she was head and servants sometimes took advantage of their mistress's ignorance.

The servants, as we have seen, had no time for such luxuries as illness. Still less had the really poor. Disraeli, writing in the 1830's, pointed out indignantly that England was not one nation, but two: the rich and the poor.

Country and town were alike sacrificed to the surge of profitable industry. After the Poor Law Act of 1834, when the Law of Settlement* was abolished, many countrymen came into the rapidly expanding towns, to look for work in the factories. Wealthy men, seeing this, found yet another source of quick money: the building of houses to shelter these newcomers. The houses they put up were a disgrace (see Illust. 14).

* Law of Settlement, passed in 1662, prohibited any villager from leaving his place of birth without a certificate of leave from the local Justice of the Peace.

14. Industrial housing in the Railway Age.
 (*From a cartoon by Doré*)

Eight   *Town Houses: The Poor*

In 1840, the Government carried out its first survey of housing. It had been stung into action by a terrible Cholera epidemic in 1832: there was another in 1849. Cholera is a disease caused by dirt, especially contaminated water, and the filthy,

35

fly-ridden conditions of the workmen's houses spread it like wildfire. Charles Kingsley, author of *The Water Babies*, and a great social reformer, wrote in his Diary in 1849:

London, Oct. 24. I was yesterday with W. and M. over the cholera districts of Bermondsey; and, oh, God! what I saw! people having no water to drink — hundreds of them — but the water of the common sewer which stagnated full of dead fish, cats, and dogs, under their windows. At the time the cholera was raging, Walsh saw them throwing untold horrors into the ditch, and then dipping out the water and drinking it!!

But the infection did not stop with the poor. Many wealthy people died of it as well. It brought home to them at last that slums were dangerous. Government Reports on housing in some of the new Northern towns gave a vivid picture of conditions:

An immense number of small houses . . . . in the suburbs of Manchester are built by the members of building clubs. The walls are only half brick thick, or what the bricklayers call 'brick noggin' and the whole of the materials are slight and unfit for the purpose. . . They are built back to back; without ventilation or drainage; and like a honeycomb, every particle of space is occupied. Double rows of three houses form courts, with, perhaps, a pump at one end and a privy at the other, common to the occupants of about twenty houses.

The struggle to maintain any standard of cleanliness was desperately discouraging:

It was often very affecting to see how resolutely they strove for decency and cleanliness amidst the adverse circumstances; to see the floors of their houses and the steps washed clean, made white with the hearth-stone . . .; to see their clothes washed and hung out to dry, but befouled by soot from the neighbouring furnaces; and to see their children . . . . notwithstanding all their care, pale, sickly, and drooping, evidently from the pestilential miasma of a natural stream converted into a sewer, and dammed up for the sake of mill-power. . . .

There was little really scientific knowledge of hygiene at that time. Flies and dirt were allowed near food; drains were in their infancy. Even the rich had no proper sewers, but cesspits under their houses, from which rose poisonous gases at the most inconvenient moments, as a certain 'gentleman of distinction' complained:

Whenever he had a party there was a stronger fire in the kitchen and stronger fires in other parts of the house, and the windows and external doors being shut, and a greater draught created, large quantities of the foul air from the sewers rose up.

The 1830's and 1840's brought some attempts to put things straight. Unfortunately, the position was already so bad by this time that it was over a century before modern standards of hygiene were general, and even now much remains to be done. In these years, Factory Acts were passed to limit the working hours of women and children, and the system of government reorganised, making it easier to carry out reform in future.

In 1834, a new Poor Law was brought in, resulting in a more efficient system, but bringing terrible hardship to the country poor in the process. The Speenhamland system was abolished. In future anyone needing relief had to go into the Workhouse, which was deliberately made as unpleasant as possible, to deter people from entering it. In the end, this measure forced the farmers to pay a 'living wage', but, until they did so, untold families were forced to 'go to the Union', the men and their sons being totally separated from their womenfolk.

The factory worker also had a sound grievance about his pay, in what was known as the 'truck system'. This forced a worker to take part of his wages in goods, usually groceries, from the shop run by the management. The latter bought cheap and often poor quality goods wholesale and charged the worker shop prices for them, thus cheating him of part of his wages. There was no option about

37

this, even if the man did not want the particular goods given. Small wonder that the early 'forties were often described as 'the hungry 'forties'.

Improvements came with Sir Robert Peel, Prime Minister from 1841 to 1846. Peel brought real help by reducing, in many cases abolishing, the customs duties of food stuffs imported into the country. The price of food at once dropped. This policy, known as 'free trade' helped the manufacturers too, as they were now able to sell their goods in other countries more cheaply. To compensate the Government for the money lost, Peel re-introduced Income Tax. This meant that those who had enough money paid the taxes, rather than the poor, who could not afford it. In 1842, when it came in, this tax was levied on all incomes of over £150 a year, an interesting comment on what was then a comfortable income. For every pound earned over this amount, the recipient had to give the Government 7d. One duty, however, remained to be removed, the Corn Law, which governed the price of bread, the poor man's staple diet. Unfortunately, Peel had promised the farmers in his party he would keep it. Faced by a famine in Ireland in 1845 and a bad harvest here, he made the brave decision to sacrifice his career in getting it repealed. Bitterly attacked by his own party and forced to resign, he made this comment in his final speech:

I shall leave a name execrated, I know, by every monopolist. . . . But it may be that I shall sometimes be remembered with expressions of goodwill in those places which are the abodes of men whose lot it is to labour and earn their daily bread by the sweat of their brow: in such places, perhaps, my name may be remembered with expressions of goodwill when they who inhabit them recruit their exhausted strength with abundant and untaxed food, the sweeter because no longer leavened with a sense of injustice.

Public health was tackled by the Government which followed Peel. Some towns, like Nottingham and Birmingham, had already passed local regulations for any new building in their area. Another outbreak of cholera in 1848 underlined the need for further action. The first Public Health Act was passed in 1848. It set up a central Board of Health in London, and empowered, but did not compel Local Authorities to set up their own. In a time of crisis, such as an epidemic, they could be forced to do so. These Local Boards were to compel householders to provide house drains, to supply a sufficient quantity of water, and to appoint a surveyor and inspector of nuisances. If they wished, they could also make local rules about removal of dirt, pave the streets, change the sewers and provide parks for general use. It was a mild measure by modern standards, but it caused wild outcries among the ratepayers of the day.

Nine   1851: The Great Exhibition

To the outside world England was on the crest of the wave. With an unrivalled fleet, Lord Palmerston, the Foreign Secretary, bullied every nation into doing his will. The year 1851 reached a pinnacle of achievement.

First came the Census of population. Such countings of the people were comparatively modern: the first had been made in 1801. Before then it had been generally feared that to do such a thing would be to tempt Providence to bring some frightful disaster upon the country for showing such vanity. The 1851 figures were very significant: of the total of 18,055,648, more than 50% were shown to live in towns. For the first time, the majority of English people were town dwellers, with all that that implies.

The Great Exhibition epitomized the new England. Despite many early doubts, it proved a national festival of achievement. Sixty years ahead of all other nations, British exhibits easily filled half of the great Crystal Palace to over-flowing. By comparison, many of the foreign exhibits were miserably primitive and sparse.

The Exhibition building itself, a fairy-tale palace of glass, was an engineering triumph and the first pre-fabricated building of pre-cast iron girders and glass was the creation of Joseph Paxton, officially Head Gardener to the Duke of Devonshire. Small wonder now that Sir Robert Peel had made it possible by repealing the old Window Tax of 1695 and removed the duties on glass, there was a great fashion for greenhouses and glass conservatories built onto the sides of houses. From a health point of view also the gain was enormous, now that light and air in a building were free of tax.

The displays in the building were our opportunity to show off shamelessly, whether in the department of machinery, steam engines, horse-carriages, jewels, workmen's model houses, furniture or just general gadgetry. Prizes and medals were awarded for the best exhibits.

In connection with housekeeping, the following awards are important: an 'apparatus for artificial ice' from France, an enamelled frying pan from the United Kingdom, a knife-cleaning machine (later much recommended by Mrs. Beeton), cast iron water closets one of which was described as 'self-acting', and a formidable rival to the cast-iron cooking range of the eighteenth century in the form of a gas cooker to provide meals for a hundred people at a time (see Illust. 15). In the latter, a new form of power was announced. The Commissioners awarding the medals had this to say about its efficiency:

The contrivances recently invented for cooking and heating by gas, of which a considerable number are exhibited on the British side, appear to be well made and constructed. . . .The chief advantage professed by them is economy . . . . but it would appear as yet, more unquestionable success had been attended to application of gas to to warming apartments, than to cooking or heating water for baths.

COOKING BY GAS.

592.—GAS-COOKING can scarcely now be considered a novelty,—many establishments, both small and large, have been fitted with apparatus for cooking by this mode, which undoubtedly exhibits some advantages. Thus the heat may be more regularly supplied to the substance cooking, and the operation is essentially a clean one, because there can be no cinders or other dirt to be provided for. Some labour and attention necessary, too, with a coal fire or close stove, may be saved; and, besides this, it may, perhaps, be said that culinary operations are reduced, by this means, to something like a certainty.

593.—THERE ARE, HOWEVER, WE THINK, MANY OBJECTIONS to this mode of cooking, more especially when applied to small domestic establishments. For instance, the ingenious machinery necessary for carrying it out requires cooks perfectly conversant with its use, and if the gas, when the cooking operations are finished, be not turned off, there will be a large increase in the cost of cooking, instead of the economy which it has been supposed to bring. For large establishments, such as some of the immense London warehouses, where a large number of young men have to be catered for daily, it may be well adapted, as it is pretty certain that a slight increase in the supply of gas necessary for a couple of joints, may serve equally to cook a dozen dishes.

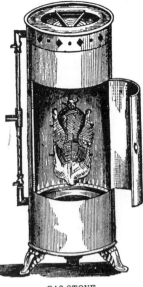

GAS-STOVE.

15. Mrs Beeton's comments (1859) on cooking by gas.
   (*Part of a page from the first edition*)

A considerable number of gas mantles were shown for lighting, an innovation which rapidly caught on. These mantles were hoods fixed round the gas jets which, when set alight, glowed brightly.

One novelty hailed joyfully by the demurely dressed ladies who came was that of the crinoline. This was a frame of hoops made of coiled wire, such as is used in watch springs, which formed a stiff but flexible bell-shape to support the full, tiered

41

16. Victorian domestics.
(*Punch Almanack, 1862*)
Notice the maid's crinoline. The chimney sweep is a reminder of the coal dust which added to her work.

17. An 1862 sewing machine.

skirts of the period. No longer, in stifling summer weather, need one endure seven petticoats, of which one had to be flannel, in order to achieve the full rounded shape of 1851 fashions. The crinoline became widely popular, lasting much longer than most passing crazes, partly because it swung lightly as the wearer walked and was comfortable. Even the servants, to the disgust of their mistresses, wore them (see Illust. 16). They could be a menace to a well-filled Victorian drawing-room.

Another exhibit was also to have a great effect on clothes. though it took longer to be accepted than the crinoline. This was the sewing machine. The famous Singer firm produced their first model for the exhibition (see Illust. 17). The days of laboriously hand-sewn seams were now numbered. Clothes became even more elaborate, as the machine quickly added frills and trimmings (see Illust. 18). But it did not come into use until the 1860's, as a careful comparison of the first and second editions of Mrs. Beeton shows. No mention is made of the sewing machine by the lady herself in 1859. After her death a second edition was prepared in 1869, adding new information where it was thought necessary. The machine was now regarded as essential:

Where the Mistress makes her own and her children's clothes it is necessary for her to possess a Sewing Machine — necessary because time is money. With the help of this useful invention, a lady can, with perfect comfort, make and mend every article used by herself and her children, and do a great deal towards repairing and making her husband's clothes, and this without labour to herself, worry of mind, and at no expense beyond the first outlay.... For general household work, the Wheeler and Wilson, the Florence and last, but not least, the Howe, will be found the most useful machines; they are all lock-stitch, and can be had from £8. 10. 0. up to 20 guineas, according to the ornamentation of the machine. For Embroidery, the Grover and Baker takes the highest place, and is very useful when much ornament is required for children's and ladies' dresses and cloaks. For those ladies who cannot afford the outlay for a first-class sewing machine — always the cheapest in the end — a hand machine will be found a most useful aid....

43

18. Fashions for 1864. Trimmings and crinolines, even for children.

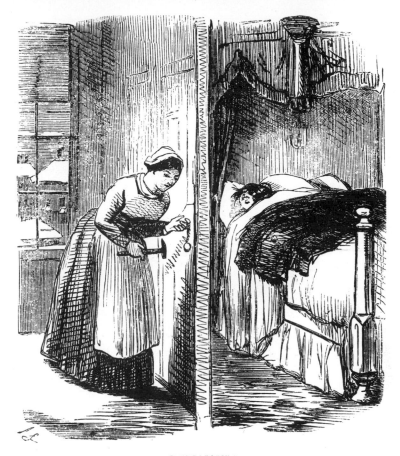

DELICIOUS !

Party in Bed. " HEY! HOLLO! WHO'S THAT?"
Domestic. " IF YOU PLEASE, SIR, IT'S SEVEN O'CLOCK, SIR! YOUR SHOWER BATH IS QUITE
READY. I'VE JUST BROKEN THE ICE, SIR!"

19. The bathing problem in 1857.
(*Punch Almanack, 1857*)
Notice the bed hangings and the maid's uniform.

Even in comfortable homes, however, a bathroom was a very
rare luxury at this time (see Illust. 19). On bath nights, a metal
hip bath was placed in front of an open fire and filled with cans of
hot water. Washing in the morning was performed at a wash-stand,

45

20. What the 'Song of the Shirt' really meant. The price of the expensive hand-made dress is the life and health of the girl in the mirror who made it.
(*Punch Almanack, 1863*)

in one's bedroom, for which cans of hot water were brought round. Sets of china jugs and basins for the wash-stand utensils are now often to be found in second hand shops, many of very attractive design.

Ten The Poor

The sewing machine might benefit the middle class housewife but it took a long time before the cheap seamstress was replaced. She belonged to a class of workers known as 'sweated labourers'

46

whose work, done in their own homes, usually in a small attic room, and paid for by the piece, was so cheap that it was not worth buying machines to replace them (see Illust. 20). A waistcoat took six hours to make for which was paid 1/6d. They were difficult people to help, for they were too poor to risk making a protest and never met each other, and unlike the factory workers, did not form Unions for their own protection. They were scandalously exploited and had to work far into the night to earn a few pence, as Hood pointed out, in a famous set of verses which he sent to *Punch* in 1843:

From 'The Song of the Shirt'.

With fingers weary and worn,
    With eyelids heavy and red,
A woman sat in unwomanly rags
    Plying her needle and thread —
Stitch — stitch — stitch!
    In poverty, hunger and dirt,
And still with the voice of dolorous pitch
    She sang the 'Song of the Shirt'.

Work — Work — Work!
    While the cock is crowing aloof;
And work — work — work
    Till the stars shine through the roof.
It's oh! to be a slave
    Along with the barbarous Turk,
Where woman has never a soul to save
    If this is Christian work!

Work — Work — Work!
    Till the brain begins to swim;
Work — work — work
    Till the eyes are heavy and dim'!

Seam, and gusset, and band,
    Band and gusset and seam,
Till over the buttons I fall asleep
    And sew them on in a dream!

Oh, men with sisters dear!
    Oh, men with mothers and wives!
It is not linen you're wearing out,
    But human creatures' lives!
Stitch — stitch — stitch,
    In poverty, hunger and dirt,
Sewing at once with a double thread
    A shroud as well as a shirt.

Other distressed people included the many street criers and scavengers with which the London streets swarmed. They were the relics of the old London 'mob' of the eighteenth century. Sir Robert Peel's Police Force of 1829, restrained their previous wild outburst of property breaking and disorder, but many continued to live squalid lives, nosing round the 'dustbins' of the more fortunate, like dogs, looking for scraps. Of this group, those who fared best were the street-traders. Henry Mayhew spent much of his time in the 1850's getting to know these people and writing down what he discovered. Charles Dickens made great use of Mayhew's facts in his novels. Here is a typical description by Mayhew of 'Street Cries', written in the year of the Great Exhibition. From it you may gather a good deal of the prices of the day:

In the first place all the goods they sell are cried or 'hawked' and the cries of the costermongers in the present day are as varied as the goods they sell. The principal ones, uttered in a sort of cadence, are now, 'Ni-ew mackerel, 6 a shilling'. (I've got a good jacketing many a Sunday morning, said one dealer, for waking people with crying mackerel, but I've said I must live while you sleep) 'Buy a pair of live soles. 3 pair for 6d.' or with a barrow, 'Soles, 1d a pair, 1d a pair;

plaice alive, alive, cheap'; 'Buy a pound crab, cheap'; 'Pine-apples 1d a slice'; 'Mussels a penny a quart'; 'Oysters, a penny a lot'; 'Salmon 2 a penny'; 'New herrings alive, 16 a groat' (this is the loudest cry of any); 'Penny a bunch turnips' (the same with greens, cabbages, &c); 'All new nuts 1d half pint'; 'Oranges 2 a penny'; 'All large and alive-O new sprats, O, 1d a plate'; 'We-ild Hampshire rabbits, 2 a shilling'; Cherry ripe, 2d a pound'; 'Fine ripe plums, 1d a pint'; 'Ing-uns, a penny a quart'; 'Eels; 3 lb a shilling — large live eels 3 lbs a shilling'.

It is interesting to discover some facts about the food eaten by these street traders :

It is less easy to describe the diet of costermongers than it is to describe that of many other of the labouring classes, for their diet, so to speak, is an 'out-of-doors diet'. They breakfast at a coffee-stall, and (if all it be yet sold) they expend on the meal only 1d, reserved for the purpose. For this sum they can also procure a small cup of coffee, and two 'thin' (that is to say two thin slices of bread and butter). For dinner— which on a week-day is hardly ever eaten at the costermonger's abode — they buy 'block ornaments', as they call the small, dark-coloured meat exposed on the cheap butchers' blocks or counters. These can be cooked in a tap-room; half a pound costing 2d. If time be an object, the coster buys a hot pie or two; preferring fruit pies when in season, and next to them meat-pies. 'We never eat eel-pies' said one man to me, 'because we know they're often made of large dead eels. We of all people are not to be had that way. But the haristocrats eats 'em and never knows the difference.' . . . On Sunday, the costermonger, when not 'cracked up', enjoys a good dinner at his own abode. This is always a joint of half-shoulder of mutton—and invariably with 'lots of good taturs baked along with it'. In the quality of their potatoes these people are generally particular.

Eleven The Challenge to English Farming

Meanwhile, the long reign of the rich farmer was about to be challenged. Britain exported everything she invented; two of these inventions were about to rebound on her. The coming of the railways to the Prairies of North America made it possible to bring vast quantities of the grain, grown on these lands, to the coast for shipping to Britain, by another of her inventions the iron steam ship. From 1875 onwards, with no Corn Laws to protect them from the competition of cheap foreign corn, the farmers were faced with a depression.

Their position was made worse by developments in the meat trade. As early as 1868, P. G. Armour of U.S.A. had succeeded in canning meat, and this too was exported to Britain. It was un-appetising stuff at first, but was popular with the poor because it was cheap. It was often the only meat they could afford at all and was a very welcome addition to their dreary food. In the early 1880's, the introduction of refrigerated ships made it possible to bring fresh meat, also at cheap prices, from Argentina, Australia and New Zealand.

English farmers could not hope to compete with the low prices and large quantities of these new suppliers. Many had to sell up. Only those who had the capital to introduce mechanical farming could hope to keep going. Combine harvesters were coming in at this time, and later tractors. Some turned successfully to market gardening. Farm labourers continued to live on a very bare sub-sistence level though cheaper food from abroad forced prices down in England to some extent: ten shillings a week was an average wage in 1890.

The first charge on the labourers' ten shillings was house rent. Most of the cottages belonged to small tradesmen in the market town and the weekly rents ranged from one shilling to half a crown. Some labourers in other villages worked on farms or estates where they had their cottages rent free; but the hamlet people did not envy them, for 'Stands to reason', they said, 'they've allus got to do just what they be told, or out they goes, neck and crop, bag and baggage'. A shilling, or even two shillings a week, they felt, was not too much to pay for the freedom to live and vote as they liked and to go to church or chapel or neither as they preferred.

Every house had a good vegetable garden and there were allotments for all; but only three of the thirty cottages had their own water supply. . . .

Against the wall of every well-kept cottage stood a tarred or green-painted water butt to catch and store the rain water from the roof. This saved many journeys to the well with buckets, as it could be used for cleaning and washing clothes and for watering small, precious things in the garden. It was also valued for toilet purposes and the women would hoard the last drops for themselves and the children to wash in. Rain-water was supposed to be good for the complexion, and, though they had no money to spend upon beautifying themselves, they were not too far gone in poverty to neglect such means as they had for that end.

(Written of North Oxfordshire in the 1880's by Flora Thompson in *Lark Rise to Candleford*, 1939).

Such a family lived on the traditional fare of centuries: bacon from the pig kept in the sty (half of which would be sold) was boiled in the big pot over the fire, together with cabbage and beans suspended in a net in the chimney. Suet puddings were also cooked in the same way. The skill of experience enabled the housewife to cook them all together in the same pot. Soup was also used to fill up (as was Yorkshire pudding, eaten before the meat course in the North). Flour was bought by the stone and baked into bread twice a week. When cakes were made, three would be made at a time. Home-made jam was produced in season, made with sugar at 2d a pound. Butter at this time cost 1/4d a pound and was used for cooking as well as on bread. Milk was 2d a pint and a large loaf (bought) 2d. Paraffin was 8d a gallon and matches 1d for a dozen books. Candles were bought in pounds and the number varied according to their quality; the better ones gave eight to a pound and the poorer ones twelve. Small wonder that, in 1898, at the beginning of the Boer War, 40% of the volunteers for military service were found to be medically unfit and rejected.

The living conditions of the cottagers were often no better than their food. In cottages in Farnham (Surrey) in the 'nineties:

Everything had to done practically in one room—which was sometimes a sleeping room too, or say in one room and a wash-house. The preparation and serving of meals, the airing of clothes and the ironing of them, the washing of the children, the mending and making – how could a woman do any of it with comfort in the cramped apartment, into which, moreover, a tired and dirty man came home in the evening to eat and wash and rest, then to potter in and out from garden or pig-stye, 'treading in dirt' as he came? Then, too, many cottages had not so much as a sink where work with water could be done; many had no water save drawn from a tap, but it all had to be fetched from well or tank. And in the husband's absence at work, it was the woman's duty – one more added to many others – to bring water indoors. In times of drought water had often to be carried long distances in pails, and it may be imagined how the housework would go in such circumstances. For my part I never wondered at roughness or squalor in the village since that parching summer when I learnt that in one cottage at least the people were saving up the cooking water of one day to be used over again on the day following.

(George Bourne: *Change in the Village*)

This was in the South of England. In the North, 'living in' on a farm was still common.

Fred Kitchen went, as a lad of thirteen to his first 'living place' as a farmer's boy, in the West Riding of Yorkshire. He has painted a vivid picture of the farm on which he worked:

The kitchen where we had our meals was a big, square place, with a stone-flagged floor scrubbed and scoured till it shone cold and bare as charity. A big solid-looking table stood in the centre, and here George and the missus had their meals, my seat being at the side-table near the door, which was handier for odd jobs. A stone slab with a pump stood near the window overlooking the flagged courtyard. Opposite the window was a wide fireplace with shining cooking-range, in front of which was a solitary hearthrug, the only bit of covering on that wide expanse of flags. There, George, the missus, and Laddie the sheep-dog warmed their toes; but never the toes of the hired lad. On one side of the fire-place hung a long-handled copper warming-pan, and on the other side stood a bright copper kettle, neither of which were ever used, and, by the way they shone, might never have been used. Two brass candle-sticks stood on the chimney-piece and a pair of brass snuffers hung under a cake merchant's almanack in the centre. In one corner stood a grandfather clock with spray of roses painted across its dial. Several rows of hams and flitches,* and a double-barrelled gun, hung from the ceiling, and that was the furnishing of the great kitchen, where everything was scrubbed and scoured and uncomfortable.

(Brother to the Ox: Fred Kitchen 1963)

It was a hard life:

The farm wasn't a bad 'living place'; there being plenty to eat. The trouble was I hadn't enough time to eat in. The missus said she 'wanted a lad to live-in for to do the odd jobs'. She kept no maid, saying she 'wouldna' be pested wi' such frauchless** wenches as ther' is nowadays', and preferred doing all the housework herself. Which was a fallacy, for that was where my odd jobs came in. From morning to night she kept me on the run doing odd jobs, so that during mealtimes I was running in and out like a dog in a fair.

(Brother to the Ox)

Twelve London Life: 1900

Even the better-paid town dwellers could not afford to be extra-vagant. In 1879, Mrs. Hughes had just married a young barrister. She had received the usual good advice from her family and friends beforehand:

Bessie of Guernsey, of mature experience, had advised me to get every-thing at Whiteley's. 'You've only got to walk into the shop, order what you want in the different departments, and you find everything delivered at your door.' She was right, but I soon found that this easy way of buying had to be paid for by too high prices, so I deter-

---

* A flitch was a side of hog, salted and cured.
** General meaning 'feckless' – Yorkshire idiom, probably derived from German 'frau' – hausfrau.

mined to explore the neighbourhood, buy what I wanted and bring it home myself.

One fortunate morning I found, quite a short distance away, another of London's oddities. It was a complete contrast to our row of respectable shops — no outward attractions and yet enjoying the liveliest trade. In an old narrow winding lane, once no doubt a medieval thoroughfare, I found shops and stalls catering for those who have no money to waste and mean to get the utmost value for their outlay. They were not to be put off with stale vegetables or doubtful fish — such as I had experienced in 'better-class' shops. . . .

One shop, a greengrocer's, was the most satisfactory place of business I have ever been in, for there seemed to be no waste at all. . . .

The premises were allowed to remain ramshackle, no books were kept, no credit given, and the whole energy of the staff was devoted to getting the best they could every morning from Covent Garden and selling it quickly at a small profit. By the 'best' I don't mean exotic fruits or anything out of season, but great piles of what was 'in' — such as fresh strawberries, raspberries, currants — served out to the first comers (often little children) with good humour, homely manners and very little wrapping up. Once I had already filled my shopping basket when I spied some sprouts and begged for a paper bag to put them in 'Not for greens, my dear' was the inexorable reply.

(M. V. Hughes: *A London Home in the Nineties*)

In the days before National Insurance and free medical care an illness or a death in the family could ruin it almost overnight. How careful people had to be, in order to save money for such emergencies, is well shown by Richard Church, in his autobiography *Over the Bridge*. His father was a Civil Servant in the Post Office and his mother a Board School teacher. By many people's standards, this family was comfortably off, yet it was a heart-rending catastrophe the day he ruined his new boots by leaving them too long in the oven of the kitchen range when they got wet. Boots were a major item for everyone.* The cost,

*Writing in 1912, George Bourne in *Change in the Village* relates: A man said, looking fondly at his children: 'I has to buy a new pair o' shoes for one or other of us every week. Or if I misses one week, then next week I wants two pair.'

in over-work, of such a life as his Mother led was very heavy:

Mother prepared the midday meal every morning before leaving for school; I needed only to add salt to the saucepan of peeled potatoes, and put it on the gas-stove. If the meat was steak, or chops, I would light the grill, and get the pan hot in readiness before Mother came hurrying home, often short of breath and flushed, her eyes brighter than they need be. Jack, who followed me home, took a share of the jobs, either laying the table, or filling the scuttle, though he was usually distrait, in pursuit of one of his creative dreams. . . .

This was in the year 1900. Queen Victoria was still on the throne.

In 1897, she had celebrated her Diamond Jubilee; sixty years a queen. The new art of cinematography was called in to record this great occasion. It expressed the modern world which the old lady had survived to see. As she sat in her carriage, drawn by the horse power of the past, she yet belonged to an era which had, the previous year, taken the daring step of allowing the horseless monster, the motor car, to travel along the roads at a speed of over four miles an hour. In her reign Great Britain and her Empire reached the summit of its wordly greatness. The splendour and vigour lived on after her death in 1901; so did many of the social problems with which her Governments had been grappling for many years.

Thirteen   1901—14: End of an Era

The first few years of the twentieth century were years of unrest and strikes. Mr. Loyd George, as Chancellor of the Exchequer, brought in a bold programme of reforms between the years 1906 and 1911. Old Age pensions were introduced: school meals were available, a wonderful help to the child for whom it was the only decent food he ever saw. Labour Exchanges were set up and compulsory medical examinations for all school children enabled the nation to begin to establish good health among its young people. There was still much unemployment, however, and strikes were common. Groups of determined women, some of whom had been interested for many years before, began to demand the right to vote. Men had slowly achieved this right during the previous century. The Suffragettes, as these women came to be called, began to get a name for outrageous and daring deeds, intended to attract the attention of the Government to their demands.* They locked themselves to the railings of Buckingham Palace and threw away the key so that they could not be taken away. They smashed plate glass windows, they went to prison and starved themselves out. Others, who disapproved of this violence, held meetings and presented petitions to Members of Parliament.

The Kaiser, in Germany, as he considered the possibilities of a European war, looked at the reports of his Ambassador from London, describing all this unrest, and decided that Britain would never come into a war at that time: she was far too busy. He was wrong. When his soldiers marched into Belgium, in August 1914, Britain joined France and Russia in opposing him, but when we emerged from the struggle in 1918, much that was traditional in the Britain of Queen Victoria had gone for ever.

Fourteen   The Twentieth Century: Period of Wars and Emergencies

The declaration of war on Germany, on 4th August 1914, was hailed with enthusiasm by many Englishmen. The threat of violence had been a constant anxiety during the previous years. Now the issue was plain and the London crowds flocked to Buckingham

---

* 'Suffrage' is the right to vote. Men asking for the vote had been known as 'suffragists'. When women began their demands, *Punch*, intending to make them look ridiculous, referred to them as 'suffrag-ettes'. The name struck and is the accepted term for members of the movement.

Palace to cheer the King and Queen and to assure one another that 'it will all be over by Christmas'. They were still thinking in terms of those remote Victorian wars which only touched the majority through the columns of a newspaper.

They had forgotten that science and technical progress can be harnessed for war and destruction, as well as for progress and peace. The Generals had not. The great Kitchener talked, from the beginning, of a struggle of at least two years duration. As it proved, the disastrous 'war to end all wars' lasted over four years. In 1918, Great Britain and her allies, France and later the United States of America, emerged the victors, but so exhausted that it took them years to recover. Britain no longer dominated the world: this position had now passed to the United States of America, which had come to our rescue in April, 1917.

The First World War completely shattered the dream of happy progress which had been accepted as fact in Edwardian Britain. The horrors of modern warfare resulted in the most tragic casualty lists the world had ever seen. New weapons, such as the submarine, the tank and gas warfare killed over a million British soldiers and over two million Frenchmen: Germany lost four million. This represented the cream of Europe's young men. In England alone, there was a surplus of a million women, over the total male population.

The women had come into their own during the war years. As men left for the front, women took their places in many jobs which had previously been regarded as exclusively male. There were bus conductresses, postwomen, and women window cleaners, not to mention the girls in munitions factories, nursing and the newly-formed women's services. This was a far better way of proving their worth than chaining themselves to railings, and they seized the opportunity eagerly. As a result there was a shortage of servants and even Society ladies, completely unused to manual work, cheerfully gave their services wherever they were needed.

Many men feared the competition from women for jobs, once peace came, and there were. some strikes against this so-called dilution of labour.

The implications of modern war took the country completely by surprise in 1914. Like Napoleon, the Kaiser promptly blockaded our ports and used his new submarines to sink the ships bringing essential food supplies in. As food became scarcer, prices soared and queues formed;

Coal soon rose in price: by February 1915 it cost 34s. to 36s. a ton. whereas before the war it had been round about 20s. Bread rose steadily: on the outbreak of war it cost, on the average, 6d a quartern loaf. In April 1915 it cost 8½d., in January 1916, 9½d., in October 10d., in November 10½d. In January 1917 white bread was banned and the making of standard bread, which included a proportion of barley, rice, oatmeal, beans, and maize and later potato, was made compulsory; but the price continued to rise – in February 1917 to 11d and in March to 1s. . . . Milk, whose pre-war price was 4d a quart, rose to 9d. in the autumn of 1917. Butter, before the war 1s to 1s. 2d. a pound, rose to 2s. 6d. Honey in 1917 cost 2s. 10d. a pound. Sugar went up from prices varying between 1½d. and 3d. a pound to 6d. and 8d. Eggs, which before the war had varied between ½d. and 1d. each according to the season, cost 5d. each in 1916, and went up to 5d. and 6d. each. In November 1916 the increase in the price of food since the beginning of the war was estimated at seventy-eight per cent.; in November 1918, one hundred and thirty-three per cent.

Not until December 1916 was it thought necessary for the Government to step in and organise food supplies. The Ministry of Food was then set up. To help the poor, the millers were subsidised in September 1917, and the price of bread thus established at 9d. a loaf. Ingenuity is stimulated by emergency and many substitute foods were brought out:

From 1917 onwards there was a real shortage of staple items of the average diet. . . . Substitutes became the orders of the day, saccharine, glucose, syrup, honey for sugar; potatoes for bread, and when potatoes were scarce in 1917 owing to a failure in the crop, rice and maize for potatoes – not the sweetcorn of the United States, but the dried maize used for cattle fodder; bacon, dried beans, oatmeal, for meat; margarine for butter, and then cocoa butter for both.

(Irene Clephane: *Ourselves 1900–30*)

For the first time in England's history, the civilian population was subjected to direct attack from air raids carried out by Zeppelins. The first raid on London took place on the 31st May, 1915. Moreover with the fearful carnage in France, everybody lost friends and relatives. As time went on, the fighting came to a virtual stalemate; each side inflicting and receiving fearful casualties, but gaining no ground. The war seemed endless, whether to the soldier in the filth and horror of the trenches, or to those who waited fearfully at home and rushed out to buy the 'Special Editions' sold by the newsboys at times when an assault was mounted, giving columns of the names of the dead. Life had a nightmare quality. As the years dragged on, with no indication of the end in sight, people asked one another, 'Will it ever end?' At last it did.

Never did the welkin ring in London as it rang today. Parliament Street and Whitehall were packed with people. The day was grey and chill with a threat of rain, but no one minded the weather. There prevailed everywhere throughout London an irresistible impulse to let business go hang, to get into the streets and yell and sing and dance and weep.

(Michael MacDonagh writing 11 Nov. 1918)

Mr. Lloyd George voiced peoples' feelings that night in Parliament thus:

Thus, Mr. Speaker, at eleven o'clock this morning, came to an end the cruellest and most terrible war that has ever scourged mankind. I hope we may say that thus, this fateful morning, came to an end all wars.

People said joyfully that there could never be another war in their lifetimes. 'Peace in our time', was the slogan with which they sent Lloyd George to sign the Peace Treaty in Paris which set up the League of Nations to ensure their dream's realisation. Some also fought the election of that year on a grimmer note: 'Hang the Kaiser'.

There was also a heavy note of revenge in the treaty.

The prevailing spirit of optimism was short-lived. Politicians visiting soldiers in France, had always assured the troops that they would return to 'Homes fit for Heroes'. The reality proved very different. The men were demobilised quickly, without any special preparations being made for their return to civilian life. They arrived back to wholesale unemployment and a shortage of houses. Strikes were frequent, but did little good at a time when the unemployed could be drafted to fill the places of the strikers. Even the General Strike of 1926, when the three great Unions of the Miners, Railwaymen and Transport and General Workers came out, ended in dismal failure. The politicians were powerless to ease the depression which caused it, for the roots of the trouble ran deep into all the countries of the world. Some attempt was made, in 1918, to tackle the housing problem. The Act of that year officially assisted local authorities to begin housing schemes to build estates on which the rents would be assessed to a working man's pocket. This was a far-sighted, but long overdue measure, and is the origin of the Council Estate.

Town and country were hit alike by the depression. The narrow margin of a labourer's budget in 1925 is well shown by the following figures:

Outlay by a Farm Worker's Wife in a week of May 1925 (from a weekly wage of 31/-) Parents and 3 Children

	s	d.
Food (21s. 0d.)		
Milk, 3d. a pint	3	6
4 lbs. Sugar	2	0
Packet of Breakfast Oats		8½
¼ lb. Tea		8
Meat, 1s. 1d. per lb. (5 lb.)	5	6
Flour, 2½ stone for six people	7	0
¼ lb. Baking Powder		4
½ lb. Lard		5½
1 lb. Rice		6

Salt		*1*
Yeast		*3*
Other Expenditure (5s. 3d.)		
1 cwt. Coal	*3*	*9*
½ lb. Candles		*2½*
½ gall. Oil		*7*
1 lb. Soap		*6½*
Soda		*1*
Matches		*1*
	26	*3*

Bread was made at home, and nothing is allowed for rent (3s.), or for new clothes or for new boots or any other renewals, repairs, chapel, paper, recreation, or savings. The wage the woman had to do with was, counting in harvest money, 31s. only. How did she manage? The secret was that, like many another labourer's wife, she went out to work.

(Robertson Scott: *The Dying Peasant*)

Such a life was a hard struggle. Yet it is clear from an article in 'The Times' of the early 1930's that it represented a great improvement on previous days:

Rural workers, alone among those who live by the land, have during the last half century prospered materially. Since 1880 their wages have been approximately doubled, their hours shortened; they are paid extra for overtime and harvest; they have a weekly half-holiday. Taking into account the higher cost of living, the rise in net income is substantial. The maximum rent that can be deducted for cottages, generally with gardens, is 3s. a week, and their homes have been made more habitable by improved sanitation and water supply. Again, since 1880 they have obtained pensions in their old age and a variety of benefits in sickness and convalescence.

The Lord Ernle, who wrote this passage and was a famous historian, points out that the old Squire is now faced with final ruin, since he lacks the means to invest in the very expensive new machinery which is now required for successful farming and which can only be used economically on very large farms. It is clear, from a book written in 1926, entitled *The Dying Peasant*, that life was still very hard for many farm labourers.

I have been staying in a lonely village under the Downs in the Isle of Wight which I have known for twenty years,' writes someone in the *Nation* in July of the present year (1926). 'The cottages are nearly all badly overcrowded. Young people marrying leave the village as a matter of course, however much they want to stay. The chief of life's terrors for the farm-labourer is illness, for the cottages are "tied" and the farmers turn a sick labourer out to make room for one who can work. The labourer's family gets meat once a week or perhaps once a fortnight. Many keep a pig and have a barrel of salted pig as a standby. The men have no holidays and are singularly patient and harmless. Out of a miserable wage they subscribe with pathetic generosity through the Union to help any labourer who is ill and unable to work. The village, like other lowly organisms, manages to exist, and that is about all'.

The man on the unemployment dole was the worst hit. Families in the depressed industrial areas had a very bleak life in the 'twenties and 'thirties, some of them for many years at a time. The following account of her childhood was given to the writer by the daughter of an unemployed cotton worker in Lancashire in the 1920's:

In our family there were mother, father, three boys and one girl. Father was a cutlooker (Clitheroe term) otherwise known as clothlooker – he examined the woven cotton for flaws and had to reprimand weavers for mistakes in jacquard weaving or careless flaws in plain material. Apart from a short period about 1923–4 I do not remember him working much – he had a lot of illness and it was the slump. He left the cotton trade in 1929 having only been theoretically in it for about the previous 5 years. I think dole money was about 27s. 6d. for the family. I do not know how much he got for Lloyd George (sickness benefit). Rent was 7s. 6d. a week.

Food was largely bread and potatoes. Bread was home-baked (cheaper and more virtuous). Breakfast was porridge with milk and sugar, midday meal was usually hot but could be a boiled egg with bread. Once a week mother queued at the butcher and came home if lucky with two-pennyworth of bacon bones, and made pea-soup for midday meal for all six. Eaten with or without bread. Hotpot and potato pie were favourite dishes — potato, onion and a little meat with or without the addition of pastry. The chief difference between then and now is that one looked at every penny before spending it, and decided what was really essential. Milk was delivered in a churn in a horse-trap, and ladled out of the churn into a jug with a measure. The housewife had to go out to the cart every morning and buy as much as she needed, rather than leave a standing order — it was always before breakfast time, and Mother would rush out without coat, whatever the weather. I remember having lumps of frozen milk on porridge, just collected from the farmer. Newspaper was a favourite wrapping and nothing was sealed. Sugar and flour were sold loose from the sacks. Butter was cut off a huge piece (56 lbs.) and slapped with butter pats. Lard also came in bulk. Shopping was slow as everything had to be weighed. There were no aids to housework and the physical labour, in addition to the mental weight of poverty was severe.

Everything was done to the clock, or it would have been neglected. Monday was washday which involved handling wet clothing from 6 a.m. to midday, washing, rinsing, blueing and starching, and drying to the right degree — if it were too dry the starch effect could be spoiled by uneven damping. Tuesday was ironing day: no non-iron fabrics: underwear of cotton, men's shirts, sheets, towels, everything had to be ironed. Curtains, always two, sometimes three, lots at each window, had to be washed regularly. Every article of furniture was polished with wax polish every week. Wednesday was the day for baking, followed by Thursday, bedroom day, when the rooms were really spring-cleaned: no running over with a vacuum and a mop. Friday the downstairs was spring-cleaned, and Saturday the windows were cleaned in the front room tidied and dusted, the kitchen cleaned (this was a daily thing) in preparation for Sunday. Sunday the children were cleaned and put into clean things.
Clothing was a problem and I was the despair of my Mother. The three boys handed garments down apart from footwear. I could not be involved in this chain and was a big expense. My maternal grandmother often supplied clothing, although she was a widow, living alone and working as a weaver to support herself. Some she had given from friends, some she got from jumble sales or second hand. Shoes often came this way — if they didn't I wore the clogs and boots handed down from the boys.

Clogs were worn by all including mother on weekdays. A Sunday dress was often supplied by the other grandparents.

For the lucky ones in work, or with private means, a new range of inventions and entertainments emerged at this time. The newly emancipated women asserted their independence in the short skirts and the mannish Eton-crop hair style. The wealthy set drank the new cocktails from America, drove fast cars, and gave wild parties. The lesser lights went to 'Tea Dances' at local restaurants, danced the Charleston and listened to the latest 'Blues' and Jazz. The United States, previously scorned as an upstart country, increasingly set the fashion. The new Cinema especially the 'Talkies' which came in 1929, quickly spread American styles of clothing and everyday life.

Domestic gadgets, like the refrigerator, were introduced for those who could afford them, and electrical appliances in general became increasingly popular after 1926, when the installation of the National Grid made electricity easily available to many homes. One innovation which affected the lives of all, rich or poor, was that of 'wireless'. In 1922, the broadcasting station known as 2LO was set up and given a licence to relay one half-hour programme a day. The early crystal sets involved manipulation of a 'cat's whisker' to the correct position in relation to the crystal. Listening was by ear-phones. Many people can recall the excitement of hearing their first broadcast, sharing one pair of ear-phones between them. Even the most distant cottages now received entertainment and news from the capital. The news the wireless sets of the 'thirties carried however, was of Hitler's rearmament of Germany and his invasion of one neighbour state after another.

The final crisis came on 3rd September 1939, when Hitler ignored our demand that he withdraw his troops from Poland, the country he had most recently attacked. At 11a.m., as the twenty-four hour ultimatum ran out, the Prime Minister broadcast to the Nation that Britain was once again at war with Germany. The 'Peace in our time' had lasted less than twenty one years.

There were no demonstrations of joy outside Buckingham Palace in 1939. No one thought in terms of peace by Christmas. Resignation and determination were mingled with justifiable fears of what to expect from the fast new aircraft which Germany was known to have built. Before the war broke out, every man, woman and child had been measured for gas masks and these were issued on the outbreak. Gas mask drill was a feature of school life throughout the war. People were expected to carry them everywhere they went, as also their identity cards.

Total blacking out of all windows was enforced by heavy fines: going out on a moonless night could be a hazardous undertaking. London and some of the industrial cities and ports sent many of their children away to the country. Some of them came from slums of a sort which most English people thought of as a thing of the past. The arrival of the 'evacuees' was, in some cases a healthy reminder that much remained to be done before we could pride ourselves on the standard of life in England.

Profiting from previous mistakes, food rationing was brought in long before food became short. From January 1940, Ration cards had to be produced for basic foodstuffs and by July, 1941 the weekly allowances for each adult were 4 oz bacon or ham, 8 oz sugar, 2 oz tea, 8 oz fats (not more than two ounces being of butter), 2 oz jam, 1 oz cheese and a shilling's worth of meat. Try measuring out these quantities in your own kitchen and you will soon see how small they were. Later, sweets and tinned goods were put on 'points', the number of little squares needed varying with the article. Bread was not rationed however until after the war on the 21st July 1946.

One of the best-kept secrets of the war was the introduction of clothes' rationing. Its announcement came as a complete surprise. Each person was issued with clothes coupons*, and had to decide how to use them on the following basis. The newspapers for 1st June 1941, carried the following announcement by the Board of Trade:

> Rationing has been introduced, not to deprive you of your real needs, but to make more certain that you get your share of the country's goods – to get fair shares with everybody else.
>
> When the shops re-open you will be able to buy cloth, clothes, footwear and knitting wool *only if you bring your Food Ration Book with you.* The shopkeeper will detach the required number of coupons from the unused margarine page. Each margarine coupon counts as one coupon towards the clothing or purchase of clothing or footwear. You will have a total of 66 coupons to last you for a year; so go sparingly. You can buy *where* you like and *when* you like without registering.

Newspapers printed various recipes and advertisements issued by the Ministry of Food (itself created in September 1939) and Board of Trade, giving recipes such as 'Woolton Pie'.** 'Make do and Mend' instructions were also given, showing us how to convert outworn dresses into pinafore frocks and similar makeshift devices. Life was drab and dull, when it was not made too exiting by bombing, but few people in the second war went as hungry as many in the first. In fact, many people previously ignorant of food values, ate a balanced, if limited, diet for the first time and the health of the nation benefited accordingly.

As in the first war, many substitute (the fashionable word was 'mock') foods and reconstituted foods were used. The powdered foods included dehydrated milk and eggs. Strange foods were often pressed into service: Spam was the best of these. Others, less appetising, including whale meat (heavy and oily) and a fish called Snoek (pronounced snook). Rice, made without sugar and

---

* Details of the numbers of coupons required for the various types of clothing will be found in the complete announcement in its original form in Appendix II
** Lord Woolton was the Minister of Food.

with water instead of milk, featured on at least one school menu every third day of the week. Later in the war 'meatless meals' appeared at least once a week: these consisted of soup and potato, followed by a small portion of pudding. The general effect was filling when first eaten, but left one feeling very hungry by the middle of the afternoon.

Meanwhile the real battle against the enemy was fought out over our heads. In May 1940, Paris fell: once again, Britain faced the common European enemy alone. The new Prime Minister, Mr. Winston Churchill, galvanised his countrymen with tough speeches in which he offered no prospect of comfort; only an example of grim determination to 'see it through'. In September 1940, Hitler's great *blitzkrieg* on England's big cities began. The small, youthful Air Force fought against heavy odds and inflicted many casualties. People living in the bombed areas got accustomed to retiring for the night to shelters, public or their own, instead of their bedrooms. Outside the voluntary Air Raid Wardens and Fire Watchers dealt with fires and casualties, side by side with the regular Police Force and Fire Brigade. Faced by the threat of invasion, men too old for active service were urged to organise themselves for active resistance. Many of them were survivors of the previous war and were only too willing to train for defence. Originally known as the local Defence Volunteers, they were soon renamed the Home Guard. Voluntary work of all kinds was done: even school children were involved in simple jobs. Every scrap of waste went to 'salvage' to be used again.

The cost of a modern war is fantastic. In 1939, Great Britain was spending at the rate of six million pounds a day. By 1945, the daily bill was over nine million pounds. Money was raised by many 'special effort' weeks, but their effect was minute in comparison with the steadily mounting national debts. Income tax rose to 10/- in the pound and Super Tax, levied on all incomes over £2,000 rose to 19/6d on incomes over £20,000. On top of this, most people had to accept some of their pay in the form of 'War Bonds'. These were a compulsory form of National Savings Certificate, but could not be redeemed until further notice. Despite our efforts, we became permanently indebted to the U.S.A., which supplied us with many essential goods. As a last, desperate measure, in 1944, Hitler let off first his new flying bombs (doodlebugs) and then rockets over London. But the tide of war had turned against him and Germany agreed to an armistice on the 8th May, 1945.

The celebrations at the end of the second war, as with its beginning were more subdued than in the first. To begin with, the defeat of Germany did not end the fighting; the Japanese war continued. This came to an end with dramatic suddenness. On 6th August, 1945, the first atomic bomb was dropped by the United States Air Force on Hiroshima. The unparalleled destruction shocked and frightened the world. What was this new force we had unleashed? For the first time, man held in his hands the means to obliterate the entire human race.

Post War Developments

Fifteen   *1945—51 : Repairing the Damage*

The end of the war, when it came, was like waking at the end of a very bad dream. To those of us who had dreaded the coming of night for many months and years, it seemed almost impossible. No more carrying bed clothes down to shelters, nor stumbling about in the inky darkness of total black-out. We planned to use the shelter as a garden shed, tore down the black screens and paper from our windows, and piled the rubbish on huge bonfires at the end of every street. That evening, everyone turned out to sing and dance round a glorious blaze, lighting the night skies for the first time for nearly six years. The war was over. But better times were a long time coming.

Once the excitement of victory parades and parties was over Britain was forced to recognise that she could not afford to lean back and simply enjoy being a victor in war. Alone of all the countries on the winning side, Britain had fought continuously, from 11 a.m. on 3rd September, 1939, to the same time in the morning of 9th May, 1945. The cost had been crippling and she now found herself deeply in debt. Before the war, she had owned £3000 million in foreign investments. This had more than met her bills for essential imports. Now, in 1945, only one third of this amount was left. The rest had been used to pay for armaments and equipment, chiefly from the U.S.A. Likewise, two thirds of her £450 million gold reserve had also been used in the war effort. Despite this, much of what we had bought from the United States was still not paid for. In addition, prices had risen all over the world and what money we had bought less than it had before. Indeed, in 1945 we really had not enough money for the day to day expenses of running the country until the U.S.A. and Canada stepped in once more and lent us £1000 million worth of dollars, to be repaid by 1952.

69

Here lay the rub: by 1952 we had to earn enough money to run the country without outside help and to pay off this new debt. No wonder the country's leaders could only tell the people to carry on working as they had done in the war.

Tired as it was, the country managed to rise to this fresh challenge. There was one great advantage: there was plenty of work for everyone willing to do it and the Government pledged itself to a policy of 'full employment'. Demobilised soldiers did not come back to unemployment, as so many had done in 1918. There were, however, very few luxuries about. Even necessities were in very short supply and, in some cases, were even scarcer than in war-time. It is interesting to compare war-time rations with those post-war.

Weekly Rations

In War-Time	In 1948
Meat 1/- to 2/2d worth	1 3 ozs.
Bacon 4 to 8 ozs.	Bacon included in meat ration
Cheese 1 to 8 ozs.	1½ ozs.
Tea 2 to 4 ozs.	
Sugar 8 ozs. to 1 lb.	Sugar 8 ozs.
Butter 2 ozs. Margarine 4 ozs.	Margarine or Butter 6 ozs.
Cooking fat 2 ozs.	1 oz.
Milk about ½ pint a day 1 tin of dried milk (4 pints) every 8 weeks	2 pints
Eggs and Oranges as available	Eggs 1

Dried eggs were also much used, though for a short time in 1946 these vanished from the shops. After angry questions in Parliament, they reappeared. Even worse, bread and potatoes were rationed for a short time in 1947. Dried potato, of an unappetising kind, had also been produced for the first time during the war. This prolonged shortage of food was partly due to the needs of the rest of Europe. Farming had suffered badly in Europe and millions of people were in danger of starvation. Emergency supplies of food and medical aid had to be rushed to these desperate people, to friends and enemies alike.

To provide more food, the Government would have had to use precious savings to pay foreign importers, thus sending money we needed out of the country again. Government posters proclaimed: 'Britain must earn her keep . . . we cannot buy anything we cannot afford to pay for' (1947). In time, the country was rewarded by the news that her exports were now higher than they had been before the war.

The average person continued to make the best of what there was. One girl who left school and went to college in 1948 recalled some of the shifts to which she and her mother were driven, in order to dress her:

Clothes were a serious problem. School uniform would no longer do and how did one get together the necessary clothes, however few they might be by present standards, for this new adult life? The answer was in my Mother's self-sacrifice. She gave up coupons to buy some of the new clothes and gave me some of her own clothes, where they were suitable. Still there were sheets to be provided, which took more clothing coupons. Finally, faced with the necessity, we found a good spare blanket, dyed it a beautiful blue, and made it into a very handsome dressing gown.

Student life at the time had many difficulties:

Our rooms had coal fires: a great joy, despite the mess they made. The snag was shortage of fuel. Each student was allowed three small scuttles of coal a week, just enough for a fire on three evenings of the week. There was, of course, much sharing of firesides. If you studied in your room during the day, strong measures had to be taken. With a flask of hot coffee beside me, I sat in my dressing gown, hugging a hot water bottle, tucked into the arm chair with my eiderdown. Friends shuddered if they dropped in to see me, but the cool air kept one's brain remarkably clear!

Food was dull and starchy, very bad for the figure, but at least no one had to go hungry. The College kept a sow and her litters of piglets sometimes contributed to the College menu, though many people mourned deeply when Cleopatra herself went the same way. Butter was issued every week, in little individual pats, as was sugar. Milk was also short, but somehow we managed to have endless coffee parties, in the best student tradition. To begin with, bread, cakes and sweets were rationed so party fare was rather restricted, to say the least.

The Government had also to tackle the housing shortage. There had been practically no building during the war and many houses had been destroyed in air raids. Many of the houses which remained were in a bad state of disrepair. As the soldiers came home, many army camps, now no longer needed, were left to rot and fall down. The sight of these rows of unused huts was too much for some homeless families. In 1946, some of them marched into the deserted camps and set up house there: these families were known as 'squatters'. After much debate, the government decided to allow them to remain in what was still the property of the War Office. There was also a big housing drive and, by 1949, the Government could claim that it had built 558,261 new homes and repaired over 140,000 damaged ones. Emergency measures included the erection of small prefabricated houses, originally limited to a life of twenty years. By the end of 1949, 125,000 of these had been put up. As a consolation for occupying these make-shift structures, the kitchens were equipped with a number of hitherto 'luxury' appliances, such as built-in refrigerators and washing-machines. All these houses were publicly owned and rented at reasonable rates. Private building was, however, strictly limited, as were alterations and repairs to privately-owned houses. Many people, for the first time, took to doing their own decorating and repairs themselves. They were greatly helped in this by the new plastic paints and distempers which were beginning to come on the market.

In 1946, the New Towns Act had been passed, by which a number of new towns, each with their own industries, were to be set up. In less than ten years, 12 new towns had come into being; they were intended to take London's surplus population. Between them, they provided over 27,000 houses and 131 factories; but London stayed as crowded as ever.

Sixteen   Social Reforms

The years 1945 to 1950 saw a series of reforms designed to protect every citizen from the many unforeseen troubles which might beset him 'from the cradle to the grave'. As already described, the Liberal Government of 1906 to 1910 had made some help available to the aged in the form of old age pensions and to the unemployed through the weekly dole. It had also set up a health insurance scheme whereby people earning small wages made a compulsory contribution, to which their employer added, giving them the right to free medical treatment in times of sickness. During the war, the National Government began to make plans for peace-time. Its conclusions were drawn up by the late Sir William Beveridge in his great report of 1942. Among the measures recommended were a free medical service for all, a national insurance scheme for all (covering injuries, unemployment and old age) and a system of family allowances to contribute to the upbringing of each child in the family.

These reforms were made law in the years immediately following the war. In future, every citizen, whether rich or poor, was to contribute towards the National Insurance scheme and to be entitled to the free services available. At the same time, a National Health Service was set up. In the past, most hospitals were built and run entirely on voluntary contributions. Doctors were self-employed and charged patients individually for each visit and treatment. Many people could not afford to see the Doctor under this sytem. By the National Health Act of 1948, hospitals became public property and were supported by national money, and the doctors were in future also paid by the state. Every citizen was now able to register his name with a doctor and go to him for help when he needed it.

The fear of destitution was now needless. The old need no

longer dread a pauper's death and the young married couple need
not fear the financial burdens of severe sickness or child-birth. In
this way many lives have been saved. One hears many criticisms
of the cost of the service and a few people have taken unfair advantage of it, but children are healthier now than they have ever been
and the British Health Service is the envy and admiration of many
of our foreign neighbours.

By 1951 a few luxuries were coming back into the shops. Clothes
came off ration in March 1949 and sweets in May 1950. The
Government felt the time was right for a National Festival. 1951
was particularly suitable since it was exactly a hundred years since
Queen Victoria's Great Exhibition in the Crystal Palace. The
Festival of Britain was designed to show that the spirit of British
enterprise and achievement was still as vigorous as its forerunner
had been. To quote the Official Handbook; 'the Exhibition tells
the story of British contributions to world civilizations in the arts
of peace.'

As in 1851, many Englishmen thought it was a silly waste of
money when the plans were first announced. There was to be a serious
exhibition of industry and agriculture on the site opposite Waterloo Station, the 'South Bank' of the Thames, with a permanent
new Festival Concert Hall on the same site, to replace the old
Queen's Hall which had been bombed. In addition the 'Battersea
Funfair' was set up farther up the river for people to relax and enjoy
themselves. There were also local celebrations in villages and towns
all over the country. Souvenirs were stamped with the Festival
sign and there was a special issue of stamps to mark the occasion.

After years of drabness and hard work, it was inspiring to
visit the gay pavilions of the exhibition, brightly painted, in many
new designs and shapes. Inside were displayed the latest discoveries,
equipment and livestock which Britain could produce. Many of
these owed their advanced state of development to the urgency of
the war effort; among them were such things as polythene, nylon

and many other plastic materials. All these had been making their way into the shops and our homes steadily since 1945 and we are now all familiar with light unbreakable washing-up bowls, sink tidies, drying racks and floor-mats. Gone is the enamelled sink equipment, with its liability to chip and its noisy clatter, and the dusty coconut matting on the kitchen floor. Plastic foam is not only used for sponges, but also as padding for cushions and bedding.

In the advertisements to be found in the Exhibition Handbooks one can catch some of the ambitions of the English people in 1951. Electric gadgets were well to the fore. One electric firm announced:

'Ours is a nice house, ours is', and went on to explain that their electric cookers, water heaters, kettles, irons and fires were to be found 'helping round the house' in 'all the nicest houses from Hong Kong to Rio, from London to Sydney . . .'. Other firms based their appeal on craftsmanship. One claimed, 'The aim is perfection . . . and better living for people all over the world.' It took 'pride in the fact that their products are saving millions of housewives from hard, wearisome drudgery – not only in Britain but throughout the world'. There could be no more welcome news to the busy housewife, even if, for the time being, she must save up for a little longer. She was only one of many who saw in the Festival some real promise at last of easier times ahead.

Alas for bright hopes! By the end of the year, the Government was forced to announce a crisis in our dollar payments. For the first time since the war, we had bought more from abroad than we had sold. We were thus faced with the fact that we were behind in our payments to the United States. There were a number of reasons for this, apart from the increase in household and personal goods bought by the general public. After the pounding of many years, our machinery was badly worn and in many cases new machines had to be bought from foreign factories. Our railways were likewise in need of renewal: both rolling stock and track had reached the end of their working lives. Despite the end of war, nations remained so suspicious of one another that we continued to make and invent large quantities of munitions and to keep up a large peace-time army. This all had to be paid for and, in the case of military spending brought no financial return.

Once again, shortages and restrictions reappeared. The Government announced cuts in imports of tobacco, raw materials and food. Fortunately, this speedily restored the position at the time, but the struggle to maintain a sound balance of payments remains a serious national problem.

Seventeen   *1952—60 : Peace and Plenty*

For all its setbacks, Great Britain was generally prosperous in the 'fifties. The period has frequently been described as the 'age of affluence'. Wages were rising steadily; so were prices. There was a great demand for 'consumer goods' such as television sets, spin dryers and refrigerators. These are expensive articles at the best of times. Few people could afford to pay for them out-right. To meet this difficulty there was a great increase of hire-purchase facilities. By putting down one cash payment (the deposit) one could have and use the article at once, while paying off the rest of the cost in weekly instalments. Clearly a great advantage in many respects, this system has its drawbacks. The purchase costs more in the end, since interest is charged on the money not yet paid off. More seriously, there is a temptation to take on more hire-purchase agreements than the buyer can really afford, especially when the instalments are apparently very small, making too heavy a burden on the weekly budget and causing people to fall behind with payments, sometimes to the extent of not being able to catch up.

Food shops also showed many changes. Deep-freeze cabinets

became normal equipment in food shops and the housewife could now buy cheaply and easily fish, fruit and vegetables at any time of the year, not just when they were in season, as her Mother had done. Such foods have often been prepared for storage in such a way that they have only to be cooked very simply and quickly before they are eaten. They are packed in hygienic wrappings in the factory and sealed so that they are free from germs.

Buying and choosing food has also been made easier. Self-service Supermarkets were built and stocked on a large scale in the 'fifties. The housewife could walk round the well-stocked shelves of goods in her own time, able to see at a glance what the shop had to offer. The shops soon found that, with all this choice, customers tended to buy more goods than they really needed. As they became successful, the shops added new types of goods to their stock including nylons, musical records and children's toys.

Labour-saving devices made it much easier for women to go out to work if they wished to. With the big demand for goods, there were jobs available in factories and offices and the numbers of married women working rose from two million in 1948 to four million in 1958. Indeed, some young women, who gave up work on marriage, now found that their housework only partly filled the day and that they were then left wondering what to do with themselves. Their mothers had belonged to the generations which had always had far too much housework to get through for many leisure activities.

In many cases, there was not even so much dirt to clean away as previously. After a particularly thick fog had shrouded London in the winter of 1952–3, some Local Authorities brought in 'smokeless zones', in which people were forbidden to use fuel which poured smoke into the atmosphere. Black, sticky soot had long been the enemy of many a housewife; she was now nearly free of it.

Eighteen   Housing

Houses also were built to save labour. If you can, try to look care-fully at a number of houses built at different times and compare them. Modern houses are usually built to make cleaning as easy as possible. They often have flat doors and no picture rails, thereby avoiding dust from settling on ledges. Floors are covered with materials which are cleaned easily and will not spoil if mud or sticky substances fall on them. Many houses built only twenty years ago are much more trouble to look after.

Another sign of increasing prosperity in the 'fifties was to be seen in the increasing number of people who took out mortgages, through Building Societies, in order to buy their own homes, instead of renting them. The arrangement was not new (the earliest Building Societies were set up in the nineteenth century) but the number of people using them at this time rose steadily. By 1959, thirty per cent of householders were buying their homes in this way.

Despite really energetic efforts to provide enough houses, all Governments are constantly worried by the shortage of housing. At first sight, this would seem strange: between 1951 and 1954, over 300,000 houses were built by the Government, and by 1955 the number had risen to more than a million. In large cities, where land is short, large blocks of flats were put up to make the greatest use of the available building land. Yet in all these cities many people are living in overcrowded conditions still. What has gone wrong?

The Census returns may help to give the answer. In 1951 there were 49 million people living in Great Britain. In 1961, there were 53 million. Where had all these extra people come from? First, many people were now marrying younger and having larger families. They were able to do so, partly because wages had risen and partly because the welfare state provided much help in the form of free medical treatment and clinics for mothers and their babies. More-over, as a nation we are very well fed and people live longer than they did even twenty years ago. In 1900 the average expectancy of life was about 40: now, it is well over 70.

Despite our complaints, we are really very well off by the standards of much of the rest of the world. So much so, that people from poorer parts of the Commonwealth decided to exercise their right as British citizens to live and work here. This movement of population to Britain has added to our housing problems, but it has also contributed to our working population and therefore to our prosperity. With the arrival of our overseas citizens have also come new foods and customs: Chinese and Indian restaurants are one example.

The Englishman is traditionally slow to adopt new ideas, especially from foreigners. With more money to spend, and better means of travelling, many people now go abroad for their holidays. They return with new ideas on food, furnishing and decorating from countries as different as Norway, Italy and Africa. Television also has introduced us to different ideas and ways of life.

Nineteen   Past and Future

We take our own lives very much for granted. Have you ever thought how they would strike a man who lived 50 years ago? Even quite wealthy people did not live in the luxury and comfort which we accept as normal. If we could go back fifty years in time, we should find ourselves in another world. How different from our own was clearly shown in a recent (1966) speech made by a man who was a boy at the time:

In the small Derbyshire Village of Sawley where I was born in the first decade of this century there was a National School and a Baptist School. There was very little education beyond the age of 13 except for those who attended the Pupil Teacher Centre in the nearby town of Long Eaton. I knew all the children of round about my own age – and a pretty rough lot we were and there were certain streets that even we didn't go down.

A former colleague of mine born at the village of Denholme, near Bradford, the other day told me a similar story. Half the women in that small Yorkshire village went to the mill, a family income rarely exceeded £1 a week, there were rows of the village into which only those who lived in them ever went. The only time that a child got out of the village was on the annual trip to Bradford a few miles away. All the children wore clogs and were expected by their parents and by the mill-owners to work at the mill, first as part-timers and then after a year as full-timers.

But the chapels — this was a different story. In Denholme with its population of 2,500 there were five chapels and they were all filled on Sunday. Children had to attend morning service, Sunday school, and often evening service as well. . . .

Expectation of life was low, infant mortality high, and diseases of malnutrition prevalent. The greengrocer in our village, affectionately known as Tunkey Burton, was the most bandy-legged man I have ever seen. . . .

When the oldest people in this room were born in 1895 there were only half of the 12 year olds at school — 4% of the 14 year olds and 1% of the 16 year olds in school.

The crucial problems against which the teachers had to battle were poverty in the home and under-employment, which made child labour cheap to the employer and a source of income to the parent. The log books of the day reveal that the sort of things which disrupted schools were death, bad weather, and the temptations of casual child labour.

Now the extraordinary thing about this is that I am talking at any rate to some people who actually experienced these things, to many others who have vivid memory of them, and to still more who have heard them told and re-told by parents and grandparents, yet they seem to us now almost as remote as King Alfred and his cakes. . . .

Since those days, that is within the lifetime of many of us, we in western civilization have undergone an amazing revolution. . . . The census figures tell us of the dramatic story. When all now in this room over the age of 35 were born there were in this country 128,000 drivers of horse-drawn vehicles and in 1961 there were not enough of them to make a separate category, but there were 41,000 radio and radar mechanics who hardly existed 30 years ago. There were 57,000 fewer blacksmiths, 27,000 fewer coachbuilders, 286,000 fewer hewers of coal. But there were 447,000 more draughtsmen, 75,000 more mechanical and electrical engineers, 24,000 more doctors, and our increased affluence showed itself in 56,000 more hairdressers, beauticians, manicurists and chiropodists.

(Sir Alec Clegg)

No one can know the future. Clearly we cannot afford to be self-satisfied however advanced we may think we are. Will our descendants pity us for the primitive conditions in which we live? Or has this push-button age reached its limit? In fifty years from now, you will be the older generation, and you may know some of the answers to these questions.

21. Kitchen ranges in the early 1900's.

Quarrying the Facts

How then, should you start investigations for yourself? The first thing to decide is what aspects and period of the subject appeal to you most. Taken over a period of two hundred years, embracing all types and classes of people, this is a formidably large theme.

General

There are many possibilities. You could, for example, take all types of housekeeping in a particular period, or one class of people through a longer one. You may wish to approach it through a particular home you know. Take an old house and recreate the type of life seen in it at different times in its history. Or old kitchens may attract you, in which case it could be fascinating to trace the changes in equipment, as new discoveries made them possible. A good instance of this, is the kitchen range, which was made possible by the developments in iron casting during the industrial changes of the eighteenth century. The first was produced in 1780. One old-fashioned housewife was not impressed by the news of its invention from London.

January 28th 1796
She told me of a cooking grate that does have an oven in which to bake beside it, which opens with a lid, where the cakes and meat can be cooked, but I doubt if it is any use. I do not think it would do as well as my big oven, where I make my bread, so shall not worry John to get me one. (see Illust. 21).

John, her husband, might be relieved to be spared the expense, but his wife misjudged the new device: the iron cooking range had come to stay, until replaced by the gas and electric stoves we know today.

Perhaps you have come across some old recipe books, or old

women's magazines and would like to make a study of these? If you are lucky enough to have a run of such books produced at different dates, a careful comparison of what they say about certain chosen topics can tell you much of the way in which new appliances and methods were adopted. In particular, the advertisements in such magazines can be picturesque and intriguing pieces of evidence. (see Illust. 22). Notice in particular the line of appeal adopted. In 1862, for example, we find the words of Her Majesty's Laundress a sufficient recommendation:

GLENFIELD PATENT STARCH
USED IN THE ROYAL LAUNDRY
THE LADIES are respectfully informed that this STARCH is
EXCLUSIVELY USED IN THE ROYAL LAUNDRY,
and HER MAJESTY'S LAUNDRESS says, that although she tried
WHEATEN, RICE, AND OTHER POWDER STARCHES,
she has found none of them equal to the GLENFIELD, which is
THE FINEST STARCH SHE EVER USED.

WOTHERSPOON & CO., Glasgow and London.
This advertisement, in a post-1945 Mrs Beeton, on the contrary is anxious to prove that *everyone* uses the product.

'ESTD. 1877
Pumphrey's
BRIDAL* icing sugar
Used on cakes and on buns,
by those of high and of
low degree. Milled by an
especial process from specially
refined sugar.
*Trade Mark registered 1896'

APPROVED ARTICLES OF DOMESTIC ECONOMY.

CAPTAIN WARREN'S PATENT
EVERYBODY'S COOKING POT.

UTILITY! LUXURY! ECONOMY!

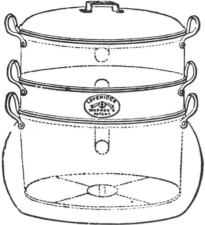

U TILITY:—So compact that meat and two kinds of vegetables can be cooked simultaneously in one vessel.

L UXURY:-The nourishing juices and nutritious properties are conserved in all their purity and richness.

E CONOMY :—Effects a saving of two ounces in the pound, or 12½ per cent. Also renders burning, scorching and smoking impossible.

GENERAL HUTCHINSON'S PATENT
COFFEE URN AND CAFETIERE.

UTILITY! LUXURY! ECONOMY!

U TILITY:—The most simple and efficient Coffee Maker yet invented. Prices within the reach of all classes.

L UXURY : — Always perfectly clear, and possessing the full aroma and pungent properties of the berry.

E CONOMY :—Perfect infusion, and the liquid may be served, even to the last drop, pure and bright.

Prices free on application to Furnishing Ironmongers in Town or Country.

SOLE MANUFACTURERS (WHOLESALE ONLY),

HENRY LOVERIDGE & Co., Wolverhampton.

22. An advertisement in the 1871 edition of Mrs Beeton's *Book of Household Management.*

8 5

You are even more fortunate if you can use family papers, such as diaries and account books. Learning to read them demands patience and care at first, but it is always exciting to read the actual words as they were written down by people at the time. In the days before the Penny Post of 1840, letters were paid for by the receiver on the basis of weight. To save money, letters were often written across the page, and then from bottom to top over the first lines. These criss-cross letters often take a long time to read (see Illust. 23).

While speaking of documents, a few words on advice on handling them should be given. Remember, these are *originals*; they cannot be replaced if they are in any way damaged or destroyed. Treat them with reverence! If you must hold a writing instrument in your hand while reading one, it should always be a pencil. Never run the risk of getting ball-point or fountain-pen ink marks on it. Make sure there is nothing which can be spilt anywhere near, especially food and drink. A cup of tea can wash away the voices which have survived for centuries. For voices they become, when you once get absorbed in the subject. The same is true of old books. Such books also need holding very carefully. Never try to open them flat; it breaks their spines. Hold them open at a right angle in your hands. The comments about marking documents equally apply to these.

Sometimes your 'original' material can be obtained in a modern printed form. Accounts such as the *Diary of a Farmer's Wife*, referred to earlier, can often be found in the Public Library. This lively young woman of twenty four started to keep her Diary in 1796. She wrote it purely for pleasure, though she wonders who in the future may read it. She is proud of her ability to write, which was not common among country people then; her phonetic spelling rings with the local dialect. In addition to being an excellent housewife, she could entertain her friends on the spinet in the long, dark evenings. She had a merry sense of humour and a kind heart.

September 30th 1796
We had a busy time taking the honey from the bees yesterday night. I and

23. A criss-cross letter.

Sarah and Carter's wife had to do it all. John saying that his fingers were very sore from burns.

Sarah dug a big hole in the ground for each skep, in which we put sulphur paper which we set alight, and put the skep (beehive) of bees on the top. The smell of the sulphur kills the bees and so we get the honey from them. It grieves me to kill the poor things, being such a waste of good bees which lie in a great heap at the bottom of the hole when the skep is taken off it, but we do want the honey using a great deal in the house for so many things. Carter's wife fell backwards and sat in a skep of bees, which made a great buzzing and sent her yelping out of the garden. At which Sarah and I laughed heartily to see Carter's wife holding up her gown as she jumped over the cabbages. . . .

Another delightful diary kept by the parson at this period, was that of the Rev. James Woodforde. He enjoyed his food and recorded every day what he had to eat.

1776, Sep. 14. Very busy all day with my barley, did not dine till 5 in the afternoon, my harvest men dined here today, gave them some beef and some Plumb Pudding and as much liquor as they would drink. This evening finished my harvest, and all carried into the Barn – 8 acres. Dec 3. My frolic for my people to pay tithe to me this day. I gave them a good dinner, surloin of beef roasted, a leg of mutton boiled and Plumb Puddings in plenty.

He also gives us some idea of the great quantities eaten by our ancestors when they could afford it, and when it was available. He described an 'ordinary dinner' in 1776 as 'a leg of mutton boiled, a batter pudding, and a couple of ducks'. In the following year, a similar meal consisted of 'A couple of rabbits smothered with onions, a neck of mutton boiled, and a goose roasted, with a currant pudding and a plain one, followed by drinking of tea'.

The account of a foreign visitor in 1782 gives a different picture of English food:

An English dinner for such travellers as I am, generally consists of a piece of half-boiled or half-roasted meat; and a few cabbage leaves boiled in plain water; on which they pour a sauce made of flour and butter.

At the same time, he had to admit:

The fine wheaten bread which I find here, besides excellent butter and Cheshire cheese, makes up for my scanty dinners. The slices of bread and butter, which they give you with your tea, are as thin as poppy leaves. But there is another kind of bread and butter usually eaten with tea, which is toasted by the fire, and is incomparably good. You take one slice after the other and hold it to the fire on a fork till the butter is melted so that it penetrates a number of slices all at once: this is called *toast*.

(Moritz)

One of the skills of this kind of work is in judging for yourself how far you can trust the evidence of the witness. Never take anything for granted. Ask yourself questions all the time. What kind of man was this? Had he any special reasons for holding the views he gave? How far do his remarks fit in with what you already know on the subject? One can only decide by knowing as much about the general story as possible. The fun really begins when you get two witnesses who apparently flatly contradict one another. It is possible they may both be telling the truth. A rich farmer in 1815 would certainly have said that times had never been better. The farm labourer, unable to afford bread because of the high price of corn, would tell a different story.

Perhaps the best way to investigate a subject of this kind is to make it a local study. This can be done, whatever other approach you decide to take. In this way, you will find information of the details you require readily available. Much of the history of the last eighty years is tucked away in the memories of old people. They have lived through a vast revolution. Much will be lost for ever if their reminiscences are not recorded now. If you can do this in another part of the country as well, through relatives perhaps, you will almost certainly notice striking differences from one district to another: a factor which, in a modified form, is still true. Life on a Devon farm is still very different from that on a Yorkshire one. If you try to talk about the whole country at once, you are immediately in danger of making very sweeping statements.

The Use of the Library

In finding out about housekeeping, the first place to visit is a Library. Naturally, you will look on the shelves devoted to History. Sometimes, they in turn are divided into different types of history: for example, that concerned with the position and function of people in society is known as *Social* history. Closely connected with it is *Economic* history, which is the study of how men used their wealth and money and of how they made it. Both can be affected by *Political* history, which is the story of how the country was governed.

Do not, however, only look at the shelves marked 'History'.

In some Libraries you might find nothing at all to help you there. Use your imagination and ask yourself, 'Where else can I look?' The Science section will almost certainly be needed for the history of inventions such as gas and electric cookers, refrigerators and pressure cookers. The 'Domestic Arts' shelves are also likely to have much to interest you. If you study foodstuffs in detail, you will also need Geography books for facts about the growing of food and the import and export of those we cannot grow for ourselves.

One very useful type of book for this kind of study is the memoir. Memoirs are just what they sound; the writer's memories written down, not necessarily in the order in which they happened, but recalling certain events and experiences which were memorable. Very like memoirs, but designed to give the complete story of the writer's life, are autobiographies. (A biography tells the history of someone else's life.)

Diaries written at regular intervals during a person's lifetime are often a vivid contact with a human being who lived and died before one was born. Good diaries and letters are the nearest one can get to talking with the people of the past. They often tell of everyday matters, fresh in their minds as they wrote: the price of food, family illnesses and disappointments, and the doings of the neighbourhood. In this book, you have already met a Farmer's wife through her diary: she lived over a hundred and sixty years ago in Herefordshire. Parson Woodforde, a farming parson in the north of England, was writing his at least thirty years earlier. As we have seen he was very interested in food and tells you what he has eaten every day.

As we have already seen, there was much experimental farming going on in the eighteenth century and some men rode round the country to see what was going on in various places. They wrote down what they discovered for the good of other farmers, so that they could try out the new methods for themselves. Arthur Young was one of the first of these. In 1767, he published his account of his journey through six counties in the South of England. He later wrote a book about a tour of the Northern counties. These are not now in print, but can sometimes be found in a large library. Other writers who travelled a great deal included Daniel Defoe who, as a Government Agent, rode all over England and told of his travels in the first quarter of the eighteenth century. Cobbett, the journalist, also described what he found, often with indignation at the plight of the poor, under the title of *Rural Rides*, in the early part of the nineteenth century. It is fascinating to look in such books to see if the writer visited one's home district, and, if he did, what he had to say about it.

Once you become interested in your own area at a particular time, you will certainly find the local newspaper full of material. Some of the advertisements alone are delightful. People lost dogs and walking sticks then, just as they do now, and offered rewards for their return. They also advertised for servants, horses, houses and tickets to fashionable entertainments. Patent medicine firms promised their readers amazing cures for their ills. In the columns of news, of course, every local occurrence is reported. Many Libraries keep copies of local newspapers and, in larger Libraries, at least one national newspaper is also kept. Most local Libraries make a point of collecting books, and sometimes pictures of their particular district at various stages in its history. Many Librarians are themselves very interested in this aspect of their work, and are delighted to show a student what they have collected.

Another type of paper is the periodical, especially illustrated ones. From the pictures in this book taken from *Punch*, you can get some idea of the mass of material to be found here. 'Punch' began in 1846. The *Illustrated London News* was another great Victorian illustrated paper. Later in the nineteenth century many more such magazines appeared, among which early women's magazines can be interesting on the subject of housekeeping, though they were mainly written for the woman who had servants to do most of the hard work. Again, if you explain what you are looking for, the Librarian may be able to find you some of these, but, since they cannot be replaced, he will probably insist on your working on them in the Library itself. Trade catalogues, listing goods for sale, can also tell you a great deal about household goods and their prices at various times.

So far, apart from biographies, all the types of books mentioned have been written or drawn by people living at the time. As such, they are original materials. What of books, printed recently, in which the writer tells you what he has found out about the past? Naturally they vary in quality. The best are those which give the facts on which the book is based. A good example of such a book for this piece of work is the *History of Everyday Things in England*, written by a man and his wife, Marjorie and C. H. B. Quennell' just before the last war. The drawings in particular are clear and accurate, showing at a glance exactly how a roof was constructed, a pump worked, or the pots and pans were used for cooking. This is because they were all drawn from actual examples which the artist went to see.

Do not be put off by the size of a book. As you get to know the subject well, you will find it unnecessary to read the whole of every book; what you need to find is anything in it which you have not previously known. Get into the habit of scanning the table of contents at the beginning, and the index pages at the end, remembering always with the latter to look under words which have a similar meaning to the ones you are seeking (e.g. 'cooking' can also be found under 'baking', 'roasting' and 'broiling'). Run your eye over the pages of text, to see if any familiar words jump out at you. This is known as 'skip' reading and is only possible when you are becoming really familiar with the subject.

Learn to use the Library catalogue. Every Library keeps a card, for each book it possesses, with the surname of the author at the top, the title, and an index number, or group of letters, telling you where to find the book on the shelves. These cards are kept, in alphabetical order, in special filing drawers. The Librarian will show you how the system works, if you ask. Once you understand it, the catalogue can save both you and him a great deal of time.

Always be on the alert for books which sound likely to be helpful. If you find a title in a book, write it down on a special slip of paper and go and ask for it. You will also find a list of titles and authors at the end of this book to start you off. The Library is your workshop. If you are doubtful about a fact, go to the Library and look it up. Take any drawings you may have made in an old house or museum and find out all about them. It is a storehouse of facts and knowledge: make full use of it.

Museums and their use

A visit to a museum brings one face to face with the objects used in daily life by people in the past. They are a solid, visible contact with their now-vanished users. Some museums display them in rooms, designed to show the furnishing of a particular date. Their atmosphere can sometimes be quite uncanny. If we look at them carefully and systematically, they will tell us a great deal about the lives of our ancestors.

Just as you have to read a book with a critical mind, so you must also approach a display in a museum. Compare similar articles of different dates with one another. See what they are made of and find out exactly what they were used for and why. Take a drawing pad with you and make rough, but accurate sketches, labelling the different parts of your drawing whenever possible and dating the object. The Curator is often very ready, especially in a local museum, to explain the exhibits and there is usually a printed guide, which you should read first. Some museums sell postcards and even little booklets about particularly interesting exhibits. A picture postcard when available can save you a good deal of trouble.

Every museum is different from all the others. None of them has the same collection of materials as any other. Naturally, the bias of a museum will vary with the objects in it, which in turn will vary with the type of district in which it exists. In some, there are displays set up as shops and these can tell you a great deal. By looking at an eighteenth century Grocer's window, you can quickly discover the goods which were available to the housewife of the period.

Remembering your original survey of a modern kitchen, look for the equivalent furniture in an old one. What was the sink like? Where did the water come from? How was the laundry done? Even better than a museum room of course is a visit to an old house which still has its original fittings. Make sure, however, that the furnishings are as old as the house. Naturally, people buy new equipment for their houses, as the latest and more efficient gadgets come onto the market. It is the job of the well informed historian to recognise such changes and to be able to 'date' styles of furniture and equipment. With practice, looking up carefully each time, this becomes an intriguing and exciting skill.

Old houses are museums in themselves. Although the mixture of ages can be confusing and upsetting, it is at the same time a necessary reminder that change is an essential quality of human life, and a man's home the best expression of the fact. As you go round an old house, however great or humble, try to imagine what living in it must have been like; dark and stuffy or light and airy; draughty and cold or warm and sunny; cramped and cheerless or spacious and comfortable. From your knowledge of the way people lived, recreate in your own mind a picture of how the rooms were used. In a small cottage, for example, there would be a constant crowd in the two or three small rooms where the family ate, slept and worked, often with the animals as well. The smell alone must have been overwhelming.

Find out where the old drains were, if there were any. The

modern bathroom is very recent and has only been generally installed since the end of the nineteenth century. Washing clothes was also an exhausting operation which started very early in the morning boiling up the water in the copper, until late at night when the ironing was done. In the nineteenth century, women's and children's underclothes were often very elaborately frilled and demanded starching and careful ironing. Even as late as 1926, wash-day was still a fearful ordeal.

Try to imagine all this as you walk round an old house. You will get to a stage where the past forces itself upon you at every turn, and everywhere you go you will find some new and intriguing details to add to your story.

History in Pictures

Looking at a picture for historical information can be exciting. It can tell you so much at a glance. It may supply the missing link between an object you have seen in a museum and its use. It may show you how the buildings in your district have been built and what the place looked like before they were put up. Old photographs, particularly if there is a set of views of the same place at different dates, can supply an absorbing story, brought together by carefully comparing the details in the pictures, in the order in which they were made.

The first thing to discover is the date of your engraving or photograph. If this is not given, it is often possible to guess it to within about ten years, by the clothes the people are wearing or by certain landmarks of which you already know the date. The title, if it has one, may also be a clue to your story: if, for example, it is called 'Market Day', compare it in your mind with a similar scene now: how was it different then? Write down all that the picture tells you of the dress, furniture, food equipment, work and lives of the people before you. How far do your notes agree with what you already know of the period? Do you think the picture is a reliable one, or has it been made to look pretty at the expense of truth?

Most pictures in the eighteenth century were bought by people who could afford such luxuries. They liked to think of the poor as happy and contented in charming country cottages, of which they only saw the outsides. It would have been difficult to sell a view which showed the dirt and overcrowding inside those rose-hung doorways, though brave men like Hogarth, even at the beginning of the century, dared to show what the lives of the poor were really like, and demanded that they should be helped.

In 1822, the Government began to take social reform seriously and more interest was taken in the lives of ordinary people: pictures of ordinary people became commoner. That is why, in this book, you will find more illustrations of the nineteenth century than the eighteenth, particularly those which appeared in the new illustrated magazines such as 'Punch', which first came out in 1846.

You will also find very few pictures for the twentieth century. This is because you should be able to find them quite easily for yourselves, in old post cards, magazines, books, papers and among family photographs.

Illustrations usually need captions: short descriptions or explanations linking the picture to the text. The captions of the pictures shown here have also been written to show how to look for information in them, not to tell you all about them.

Let us take one of the illustrations in this book and examine it in this way. Look carefully at the picture you see opposite (Illust. 24). The round breakfast table in the centre tells you the time of day, as does the father, dressed to catch his train or bus to work. What is the most important thing on the table? The large coffee or tea urn dominates everything else. If you have been looking in Mrs. Beeton, you may remember an illustration of an exactly

24. A prosperous businessman sets out for the City in 1874.
(*Punch Almanack, 1874*)
**Notice the articles on a Victorian breakfast table, and his
beautifully dressed wife, who did *not* do the housework.**

similar urn. While you have the book out look up and see what Mrs.
Beeton had to say about coffee making.

Next, let us see what we can discover about the kind of room and
furniture at that date. There is a graceful sofa across the back of
the room, with a circular mirror above it. The mirror probably has
a curved surface, distorting the reflection, but giving the impression
of greater size to the room. Such mirrors were not new at this time,
and the one in this room could either be one they had just bought
new, or one which was already an antique. Whichever is the truth
(and in this case we shall never know for certain) we have learnt
that they were in use at this time.

97

Now let us examine the people. How would you like to wear the little girl's clothes? Why do you suppose they wore so many clothes? What do they tell you about the kind of lives they led as children? The mother is beautifully dressed. It is early in the morning, but she could surely go out visiting just as she is, even to her elegant and complicated hair style. She evidently does not expect to do much housework and appears very unhurried and at ease. This was an age when servants were cheap and easy to get. We can imagine them then, waiting in the kitchen for the bell to ring from this room, a signal to come and clear the breakfast things away. Mother would then go down to the kitchen to decide on the meals for the day and to see that the work was going smoothly. She would then have the rest of the morning to herself, unless she was one of the unusual mothers who taught their own children at home. The children would be more likely to go to a small school nearby, or have a governess who taught them at home. This picture is of a prosperous, middle class family, living a comfortable and elegant existence. Once more, Mother's fashionable clothes underline this. If you were not given the date of this picture, you could easily tell, to within about ten years, what period it was. You would only have to look in any good book on historical costume, such as James Laver's *Fashion Plates 1800—1900*, (King Penguin) and you would be able to check the details of the costume, through the fashion drawings of the time. The same is true of the clothes worn by the children and their father.

Thus, when you are given an historical picture, try to make use of it as a means of stepping back into the past. Imagine you have woken up and found yourself in this room. What would strike you about it, and, if the answer is not obvious from the picture, look it up in a book on the subject. See if you can find examples of the furniture, clothing, and decorations in your local museum. You might even recognise a chair or a vase in someone's home, which has survived to now. How did it come to be there? By looking at that picture you may be able to tell its owner something about it, which has been forgotten.

Thus, you will find what you learn from books linking you with things one meets in everyday life.

The fascination of exploring the past is that it leads you farther and farther into the adventure of reliving the experience of other human beings, who only differ from oneself in that they lived in different circumstances. Some people would argue that the material circumstances in which we spend our lives change us so much that there is an actual difference between ourselves and our ancestors. Have we changed as human beings? What do you think?

Assembling the Material

The secret of writing effectively is to be quite sure what you are trying to say. This is not always easy when, after delving into a multitude of facts, you are faced with describing your discoveries in a coherent account. How are you to bring order to the assorted items of information you have collected? Obviously you cannot hope to acquire your facts in the order in which they are to be written down. However carefully you have made notes, before you begin writing them up you will have to have them sorted out and compare them with the rest.

In your final essay, you will have to do at least two main things. You must tell the story of what happened, with dates to show the sequence of events; you must also use your knowledge to show how it was that these things came about. This will require you to judge for yourself the relative importance of your different pieces of evidence. This becomes difficult if every time you wish to compare quotations, or look for a fact, you have to burrow among mountains of lengthy notes and the particular item you want is buried somewhere in a page of solid writing. What you need is a system which enables you to put your hand straight on the fact that you want without trouble.

Notes should be kept as flexible as possible. As you read, you will have to write down new facts, and you may want to quote the words of people who lived in the period you are discovering. The temptation is to take a large sheet of paper and to put down on it all the facts you find as you go along. This is fatal; not only is it difficult to sort one piece of information out from another, but many different kinds of knowledge get jumbled up together: thus, you may find a remedy for over-eating, side by side, with the butler's wages and the best way to bath baby. In order to avoid this, you may find it helpful to work on small pieces of paper, of the same size, and put down one fact or quotation on each (illustration. p. 102).

As we have already seen, within the subject of housekeeping, there are many classes of information: laundry, cookery, child-care, and cleaning, heating and lighting. Make these the headings for a card index. When you make out your slips of paper, make them to a standard pattern and size. For this purpose they should be post card size.

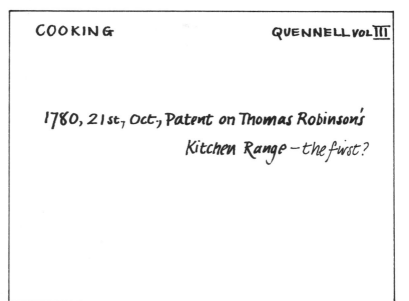

COOKING   QUENNELL vol III

1780, 21st, Oct., Patent on Thomas Robinson's Kitchen Range – the first?

First you must put the general classification heading at the left on the top line. In the right hand corner write the author's name and the page of the book from which you obtained the information. Across the centre you then write the date, if there is one, and the fact you wish to record. As time goes on, you will collect bundles of these slips, labelled 'cookery', or whatever the heading may be. Later when you are writing up the subject of 'cookery', you will have all the relevant facts in one pile, instead of having to chase, and some-times lose, them in large sheets of many notes on many subjects. The slips also help one to sort the subjects out. If you lay them all on a flat surface, you will probably be able to see very quickly what to describe first. Pick that up and then look round for the next step in the story. Pick that up and put it behind the first, as in a pack of cards. Go on picking up slips until you have in your hand a carefully organised set of facts. You can then begin to write, starting with the first note, then taking up the second and so on right through the pile.

Here, you may object that there are some sections of notes and quotations which will run into too great a length for this method. In that case, take them down on a suitable sheet of paper but also make out one of the small sheets thus:

COOKING

See Full Notes on 'Kitchens' from
Quennell 'Every day Things...' vol III

This is known as a cross-reference card and can then go into the main pack. Never put more than one note on any sheet of paper. You will often find that the notes you have on that subject also have a bearing on those of another, e.g. facts about the kitchen range, filed under 'cookery', will also be needed perhaps under 'laundry' for the heating of water.

It is also a good plan to keep a detailed date chart and to keep it filled up as you go along with your reading. It takes little time to make such an entry when you first read it in the book, but may take a very long time to find again if you come back to look for it later. The best plan for a date chart is to use lined paper and to allow one line for each year, whether you have an entry for every year or not. Enter the years in the margin on the left hand side of the paper. It is often helpful to split your page into several columns, using each for a different kind of information. Thus, on housekeeping, if you are tackling it from a local angle, you should have one column for local events, one for national ones, and one for anything with a direct bearing on housekeeping, such as a rise in taxes on food-stuffs, or the invention of a new domestic gadget like the sewing machine. When this is complete, it is often surprising how much it shows you, at a glance, of causes and effects.

It may also be necessary to make some special notes on particular subjects; for example, short biographies of people who wrote at the time and whose work you are using. These will have to be made on large pieces of paper and, instead of one fact at a time, you will have to record the set of facts which went to make up their lives. Try, even so, to keep all the biographies you make on similar lines. Certain basic facts are essential; names, dates, where they lived, and the main reasons why they are remarkable. Look particularly for facts which will explain their special viewpoints on contemporary problems. Where were they brought up and educated? All these points are important when you are judging how reliable they are as witnesses. Remember, the intelligent person always asks 'Why?' The same applies to any interview you may have with living witnesses. Such notes should be kept together, so that you can find them at once when you want them and cross reference card added to the main pack.

Illustrations and diagrams are a special source of their own. Label them neatly and fully, always making sure you have added

DATE CHART

Year	Abroad	Home	Local
1780		Robinson's Range	
1			
2		Watt's rotary engine	
3	Loss of American Colonies	Rollers for stamping patterns	
4		Cart's puddling process	Village Sunday School
5			Death of Squire George
6			
7		Cartwright's Power Loom	
8			
9	French Revolution	1st Steam Mill in Lancs	Bad Harvest
1790			
1		Tax on Wheat/ Canal mania	
2		Cotton Gin invented	Canal built
3	Napoleonic War began		
4			
5		Speenhamland System	
6			
7		Mutiny of the Nore	72, High Street built
8		Income Tax introduced	
9			
1800			

Local dates have been invented for this chart, to show how the entries should be made.

a note of where they came from. If you have many, sort them into subjects, and keep these sets separately, whether in envelopes or tied up in bundles, with a label on the outside, thus; 'kitchen ranges', or 'utensils'.

Every now and then, take a rough piece of paper and write down in headings all the items of information you have on a particular subject. It will surprise you how quickly it mounts up. Making such a list will also show you the gaps in your knowledge so far and suggest the next step to take.

When we turn to the history of the last eighty years, we can ask for details from people who remember them in their own lives. In recording the memories of old people, you can contribute to the historical records of the future. Sometimes they can produce old photographs and long-cherished possessions which, like the museum, illustrate what they are saying vividly.

Naturally, the value of what you are told will vary with the person. If you know someone has a very bad memory, it is at least advisable to check their facts if you can. On the other hand, old people can often remember details of their youth, with amazing correctness, while they completely jumble the events of the past forty years. In any case, it is a good idea to make a list in advance of the questions you want to ask. The writer compiled the following questionnaire for this purpose:

1. Where did the family live? How many in family? What was the Father's occupation?
2. Describe a day in the life of the Mother, beginning when she got up and explaining each thing in order as she did it.
3. What kind of food was eaten as a general rule? How much?
4. How big was the house? Which rooms were heated and how? How were they lighted? (Can you describe any special routines connected with lighting and heating? Baths and washing? Baking?)

5. What did you do in the evenings? What time did you go to bed and what time did you get up? Any special toys?

6. What did you all wear? How much of it was made at home? What was distinctive about it, compared with now?

7. What duties did the children have in the house and garden? Did Father ever help in the house and did the brothers?

8. What shops were near and usually used? Any comments about them? Do you remember any prices? Did your Mother have a 'Mrs. Beeton', or some similar book? What did she think of it?

9. What do you think are the greatest differences between life then and now?

This kind of work often calls for tact and patience. One has to decide what questions may be resented, for example, and discard them if necessary. You may find that some people are put off if you sit in front of them with pen and note book poised in your hands and you may have to put your writing materials aside and listen hard instead. Some time, as soon after the interview as possible, you must write down exactly what you have been told, making it quite clear what period the person is describing and what part of the country. A tape-recorder could be very useful if you had access to one, but it is only fair and polite to ask permission before using it and some people may object. Whatever happens, their wishes must be respected. Always be sure to thank people suitably for any help they may give you.

At last, when you are quite sure you have exhausted all possible lines of enquiry, you will sit down to record the results of your work. How on earth are you to bring order to such a chaotic collection of odd details? Do not be dismayed. Forget the wide range of the whole subject and concentrate on one section of it. Here you will have to decide whether to write a straightforward account of events as they happened (the chronological approach), or whether to take one aspect of housekeeping at a time, and tell the story of each in small sections. Even if you decide on the first method, you will find it drops into definite periods, enabling you to tackle a topic of reasonable size. If you work from one section to another in this way you should find it reasonably simple to gather together all the slips which contain the facts which you need.

If you can, write on one side of the paper only. If you later find you have left anything out, it is then possible to put in the missing section on the back of the previous sheet and to show by means of an arrow, where it should go in the text. Always leave a wide margin. Not only does it improve the appearance of your work, but it is also essential if you are going to bind it into a cover when you have finished. If you use quotations, and these are the life-blood of real history, they should always be between quotation marks. If it is a long passage you are quoting, the whole passage should be slightly indented (i.e. written slightly farther in from the margin than the main text). If it is really too long to quote in full, but interesting in its own right, you may wish to put a quotation in an Appendix at the end of the work. Always acknowledge your quotations by giving the author or speaker and the name of the book from which it is taken. Wherever possible, refer to any pictures you may have, which illustrate your work; mount them and insert them as near as possible to the page on which they are mentioned. Always give them a title and their source. Never stick any old engraving or map on to a paper, but mount it, either through slits on the mount, or buy some photograph corners for the purpose.

The pages of your text should be numbered, as should the pages of illustrations in a different style. Finally, when all is complete make a title page and table of contents to go at the beginning, and place the completely assembled work in a suitable cover. This need not be elaborate; a stiff sheet of folded cartridge or thin card does very well; with staples driven through, the whole can look very workman-like. The title should be neatly written or typed on the outside. Attention to small details gives you a sense of achievement and the reader is attracted to your work from the start.

Appendix I

'The Number and Description of Servants Usually Employed':

£100 a year
: a widow or other unmarried lady may keep a young maid at a low salary, say, from five to ten guineas a year;

£150–£180
: a gentleman and lady without children may afford to keep a better servant maid at about ten or twelve guineas;

£200
: *ditto*, a professed servant maid of all work at from twelve to fourteen guineas;

£300
: *ditto*, with one, two or three children, two maid servants;

£400
: *ditto, ditto*, three female servants, or two and a boy; viz. a cook, housemaid and nursery maid, or else, instead of the latter, a boy; with gardener occasionally.

£500–£600
: a gentleman and lady with children: three females and one man; viz. a cook, housemaid and nursery maid or other female servant; with a livery servant as groom and footman. A gardener occasionally.

£600–£750
: *ditto, ditto*, three females and two men; viz. a cook, housemaid and another female servant; a footman and groom who may assist in garden; and a gardener occasionally.

£1000–£1500   *ditto, ditto,* four females and three men; viz. a cook, two housemaids, a nursery maid or other female servant; a coachman, footman and a man to assist in the stable and garden;

£1500–£2000   *ditto, ditto,* six females and five men; viz. a cook, housekeeper, two housemaids, kitchen maid and nursery maid or other female servant; with a coachman, groom, footman, gardener and an assistant in the garden and stable;

£2000–£3000   *ditto, ditto,* eight females and eight men; viz. a cook, lady's maid, two housemaids, nurse, nursery maid, kitchen maid and laundry maid; with a butler, valet, coachman, two grooms, a footman and two gardeners;

£3000–£4000   *ditto, ditto,* nine females and eleven men; viz. a housekeeper, cook, lady's maid, nurse, two housemaids, laundry maid kitchen maid and a nursery maid; with a butler, coachman, two grooms, valet, two footmen, two gardeners and a labourer.

£4000–£5000   *ditto, ditto,* eleven females and thirteen men; viz. a housekeeper, cook, lady's maid, nurse, two housemaids, laundry maid, still-room maid, nursery maid, kitchen maid and scullion; with a butler, valet, house steward, coachman, two grooms, one assistant groom, two footmen, three gardeners and a labourer.

(From Mr. & Mrs. S. Adams: *The Complete Servant* 1825)

Appendix II

Exercise in Rationing

Imagine what your feelings would be if you were to pick up the newspaper tomorrow morning to find the news given here. Read the passage through carefully: then try to plan a year's clothing using the 66 coupons allowed. Can you think of any ways in which you could either make your existing clothes last longer or use scraps to make 'new' ones? Good needlewomen, who could use their materials with imagination, were at a great advantage during this time.

RATIONING
of Clothing, Cloth, Footwear
from June 1, 1941.

Rationing has been introduced, not to deprive you of your real needs, but to make more certain that you get your share of the country's goods — to get fair shares with everybody else.

When the shops re-open you will be able to buy cloth, clothes, footwear and knitting wool *only if you bring your Food Ration Book with you.* The shopkeeper will detach the required number of coupons from the unused margarine page. Each margarine coupon counts as one coupon towards the purchase of clothing or footwear. You will have a total of 66 coupons to last you for a year; so go sparingly. You can buy *where* you like and *when* you like without registering.

NUMBER OF COUPONS NEEDED

Men and Boys	Adult	Child	Women and Girls	Adult	Child
Unlined mackintosh or cape	9	7	Lined mackintoshes or coats (over 28 in. in length)	14	11

Other mackintoshes, or raincoat, or overcoat	16	11	Jacket or short coat (under 28 in. in length)	11	8
Coat, or jacket, or blazer or like garment	13	8	Dress, or gown, or frock—woollen	11	8
Waistcoat, or pull-over, or cardigan or jersey	5	3	Dress, or gown, or frock – other material	7	5
Trousers (other than fustian or corduroy)	8	6	Gym tunic, or girl's skirt with bodice	8	6
Fustian or corduroy trousers	5	5	Blouse, or sports shirt, or cardigan, or jumper	5	3
Shorts	5	3	Skirt or divided skirt	7	5
Overalls, or dungarees, or like garment	6	4	Overalls or dungarees, or like garment	6	4
Dressing gown or bathing gown	8	6	Apron or pinafore	3	2
Night-shirt or pair of pyjamas	8	6	Pyjamas	8	6
Shirt, or combinations – woollen	8	6	Nightdress	6	5
Shirt, or combinations – other material	5	4	Petticoat, or slip, or combination, or cami-knickers	4	3
Pants, or vest, or bathing costume, or child's blouse	4	2	Other garments, including corsets	5	2
Pair of socks or stockings	3	1	Pair of stockings	2	1
Collar, or tie, or pair of cuffs	1	1	Pair of socks (ankle length)	1	1
Two handkerchiefs	1	1	Two handkerchiefs	1	1
Scarf, or pair of gloves or mittens	2	2	Scarf, or pair of gloves, or mittens or muff	2	2
Pair of slippers or galoshes	4	2	Pair of slippers, boots or shoes	5	3
Pair of boots or shoes	7	3			
Pair of leggins, gaiters, or spats	3	2			

CLOTH. Coupons needed per yard depend on the width. For example, a yard of woollen cloth 36 inches wide requires 3 coupons. The same amount of cotton or other cloth needs two coupons.

KNITTING WOOL 1 coupon for two ounces.

THESE GOODS MAY BE BOUGHT *WITHOUT* COUPONS

Children's clothing of sizes generally suitable for infants less than 4 years old. Boiler suits and workmen's bib and brace overalls. Hats and caps. Sewing thread. Mending wool and mending silk. Boot and shoe laces. Tapes, braids, ribbons and other fabrics of 3 inches or less in width. Elastic. Lace and lace net. Sanitary towels. Braces, suspenders and garters. Hard haberdashery. Clogs. Black-out cloth dyed black. All second-hand articles.

SPECIAL NOTICE TO RETAILERS

Retailers will be allowed to get fresh stocks of cloth up to and including June 28th, of other rationed goods up to and including June 21st, WITHOUT SURRENDERING COUPONS. After those dates they will be able to obtain fresh stocks only by turning in their customers' coupons. Steps have been taken, in the interest of the smaller retailers, to limit during these periods the quantity of goods which can be supplied by a wholesaler or manufacturer to any one retailer, however large his orders. Further information can be obtained from your Trade Organisations.

ISSUED BY THE BOARD OF TRADE.

Some Suggestions for Reading

Reference Books and Special Studies

Reference books are designed to give factual information quickly and easily and are not intended to be read as a whole.

BOVILL, E. W.: *English Country Life 1780—1830*, Oxford, 1962.

BAYNE-POWELL, Rosamund: *Housekeeping in the eighteenth century*, Murray, 1965.

EDWARDES-REES, D. M.: *Family Life*, Blackwell, 1962.

ELLACOTT, S. E.: *The Story of the Kitchen*, Methuen, 1960.

*FASTNEDGE, R.: *English Furniture Styles 1500—1830*, Pelican, 1955.

HARRISON, M. M.: *Food*, Ward Lock, 1958.

Homes, Ward Lock, 1960.

HARSTON, Katherine: *Yesterday*, Allen & Unwin, 1961.

*HAYNES, E. Barrington: *Glass through the Ages*, Pelican, 1959.

HENDERSON, A.: *The Family House in England*, Phoenix, 1964.

HOLE, Christina: *English Home Life 1500—1800*, Batsford, 1947.

MOSS, P.: *Meals Through the Ages*, Harrap, 1958.

*PEVSNER, N. (Editor): *The Buildings of England*, Penguin. Covered in Counties.

POTTER, M. A.: *Interiors,* John Murray, 1957.

QUENNELL, M. & C. H. B.: *History of Everyday Things in England*, Volumes III and IV, Batsford, 1933—4.

REDMAYNE, Paul: *Britain's Food*, Murray, 1963.

*ROWNTREE, Diana: *Interior Design*, Penguin, 1965.

SAVAGE, George: *Porcelain through the Ages*, Cassell, 1961.

*SCOTT-THOMSON, Gladys: *Family Background*, Jonathan Cape, 1949.

TAYLOR, Gerald: *Silver*, Pelican, 1956.

* WRIGHT, Lawrence: *Clean & Decent*, Routledge & Kegan Paul, 1960. A History of the bathroom.
Warm and Snug, Routledge & Kegan Paul, 1962. A History of bedding.
Home Fire's Burning, Routledge & Kegan Paul, 1964. A History of heating.

General Accounts of the Period

BRYANT, Arthur: *The Age of Elegance*, Collins, 1950.
* GEORGE, M. Dorothy: *England in Transition*, Pelican, 1953. Changes in England in the 18th century.
GREGG, Pauline: *A Social and Economic History of England 1760–1955*, Harrap, 1964.
* HAMMOND, J. F. & B.: *The Bleak Age*, Pelican, 1934. The effects of industry on 19th century town.
READER, W. J.: *Life in Victorian England*, Batsford, 1964.
* TREVELYAN, Sir George M.: *Illustrated English Social History*, Volumes III & IV Pelican, 1964.
WHITE, R. J.: *Life in Regency England*, Batsford, 1963.
WILLIAMS, E. N.: *Life in Georgian England*, Batsford, 1962.
* YOUNG, G. M.: *Portrait of an Age*, O.U.P., 1936.

Original Sources

These are the life-blood of history; the accounts written at the time by those involved in the events. They can take many forms: books, diaries, accounts of travel, business documents (archives), letters, bills, magazines and newspapers. The illustrations and advertisements in the latter sometimes tell more than the journal itself. Pictures, especially cartoons and book illustrations, will also tell much of the age in which they were drawn. The eye-witness reports listed below can all be obtained in printed form.

THE MARCHIONESS OF BATH: *Before the Sunset Fades*, The Longleat Estate Company, 1951.

BEETON, Isabella: *Mrs. Beeton's Household Management*, Ward Lock. First Edition 1859, when the writer was 23. There have been a number of quite new editions since: make sure you know which one you have!

BURNETT, John: *Plenty & Want*, Nelson, 1966.

BOURNE, George: *Change in the Village*, Duckworth, 1912.

CHURCH, Richard: *Over the Bridge*, Heinemann, 1955.
    A London family early in this century.

*COOPER, Lady Diana: *The Rainbow Comes and goes*, Penguin 1965.
    Some interesting details of life in the great house of Belvoir in the early 20th century.

DAVIES, Stella: *North Country Bred*, A family chronicle, Routledge and Kegan Paul, 1963.

Diary of a Farmer's Wife 1796–1797, Countrywise Books, 1964.
    A Diary kept by a young woman of 24 on a farm in Herefordshire for 18 months.

*HOGGART, Richard: *The Uses of Literacy*, Chatto and Windus, 1957.

HUGHES, M. V. *A London Family 1870–1900*, O.U.P., 1946.
    Section III describes her early days of housekeeping in London in the early 1890's.

IREMONGER, Miss (Ed. Bamford F.) *Dear Miss Heber*, Constable, 1936. Letters written in the 1780's.

* KITCHEN, Fred: *Brother to the Ox*, Dent 1963.
The life of a farm labourer in the West Riding of Yorkshire, from his apprenticeship days in 1904.

KNYVETON, John (Edited and narrated by Gray, Ernest): *Man Midwife*, Robert Hale, 1946.
The diary of an 18th century London Doctor.

* LEE, Laurie: *Cider with Rosie*, Hogarth, 1959.
Village life in the Cotswolds early in this century.

* MITFORD, Mary Russell: *Our Village*, Everyman, 1965.
Reports on a Hampshire Village in about 1819.

MAYHEW, Henry (Edited Quennell, Peter)
Mayhew's London (1851), Spring Books, 1965. A horrifying, but exact account of life among the street poor at the time of the Great Exhibition. Charles Dickens, the novelist, used much of this material for his accounts of poverty in London.

* RAVERATT, Gwen: *Period Piece*, Faber & Faber, 1952.

* STURT, George: *The Wheelwright's Shop,* C.U.P. 1923.

THOMPSON, Flora: *Lark Rise to Candleford*, World's Classics. 1939. A village in Oxfordshire in the 1880's.

WOODFORDE, Parson: *The Life of a Country Parson 1758– 1802*, World Classics, 1949.
The journal of a country parson living in Yorkshire in the second half of the 18th century.

WILBRAHAM, A.: *The Englishman's Food*, Jonathan Cape, 1958.

Records of Travel

(Good sources to look for facts about your district, if the writer visited it)

COBBETT, William: *Rural Rides*, Everyman, 1957.
England in the first thirty years of the 19th century.
DEFOE, Daniel: *A Tour Thro'. . . Great Britain* (1724), Every
man 1957, (with *Tour of Scotland*)
YOUNG, Arthur: *Six Weeks Tour of Six Counties* (1767).

Mainly Pictures

BOTT, Alan and CLEPHANE, Irene: *Our Mothers*, Gollancz,
1932. From contemporary prints of women's lives 1870–1900.
CLEPHANE, Irene: *Ourselves 1900–1930*, Bodley Head, 1933.
DAVIS, Frank: *A Picture Book History of Furniture*, Studio Vista,
1962.
GEFFRYE MUSEUM Booklets and Post Cards (List available
from the Museum)
HARRISON: M. M: *Picture Source Books of Social History*, Allen
and Unwin. Volumes on: *The Eighteenth Century*
   The Early Nineteenth Century
   The Late Nineteenth Century
DONCASTER, I: (Editor) 'Evidence in Pictures Series' Long-
mans. *Social Conditions of England 1760–1830*
Victorian England 1851–1900
* LANCASTER, Osbert: *Pillar to Post*, Murray, 1938.
Homes Sweet Homes, Murray, 1939.

Books marked * are available in paperback editions.